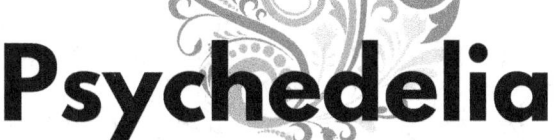

Psychedelia

Psychedelics trigger inner spirit/expression with bright and rich visual contents. You may for instance experience highly complex optical patterns, otherworldly landscapes and mysterious beings — some angelic; others demonic. Colours are frequently perceived as being extremely intense and objects may transform into the bizarre fractal and unthinkable shapes. Visions like these are a great interest to the people who seek for consciousness, peace and independent form of thinking. Plenty of artists, especially writers and musicians are into psychedelics as it helps them to form a different perspective.

Instructions (Not mandatory)

- Use bright colors (Eg: Middle Yellow, Vivid Red, Malachite, Shocking Pink, Interdimensional Blue and Turquoise Blue).
- Try not to miss the glitch and distortion whether its appropriate.
- Paint/Color it yourself and dont complain!

Your thoughts are seeds
Brain is the Garden
Acid is the Fertilizerish

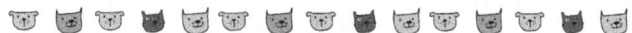

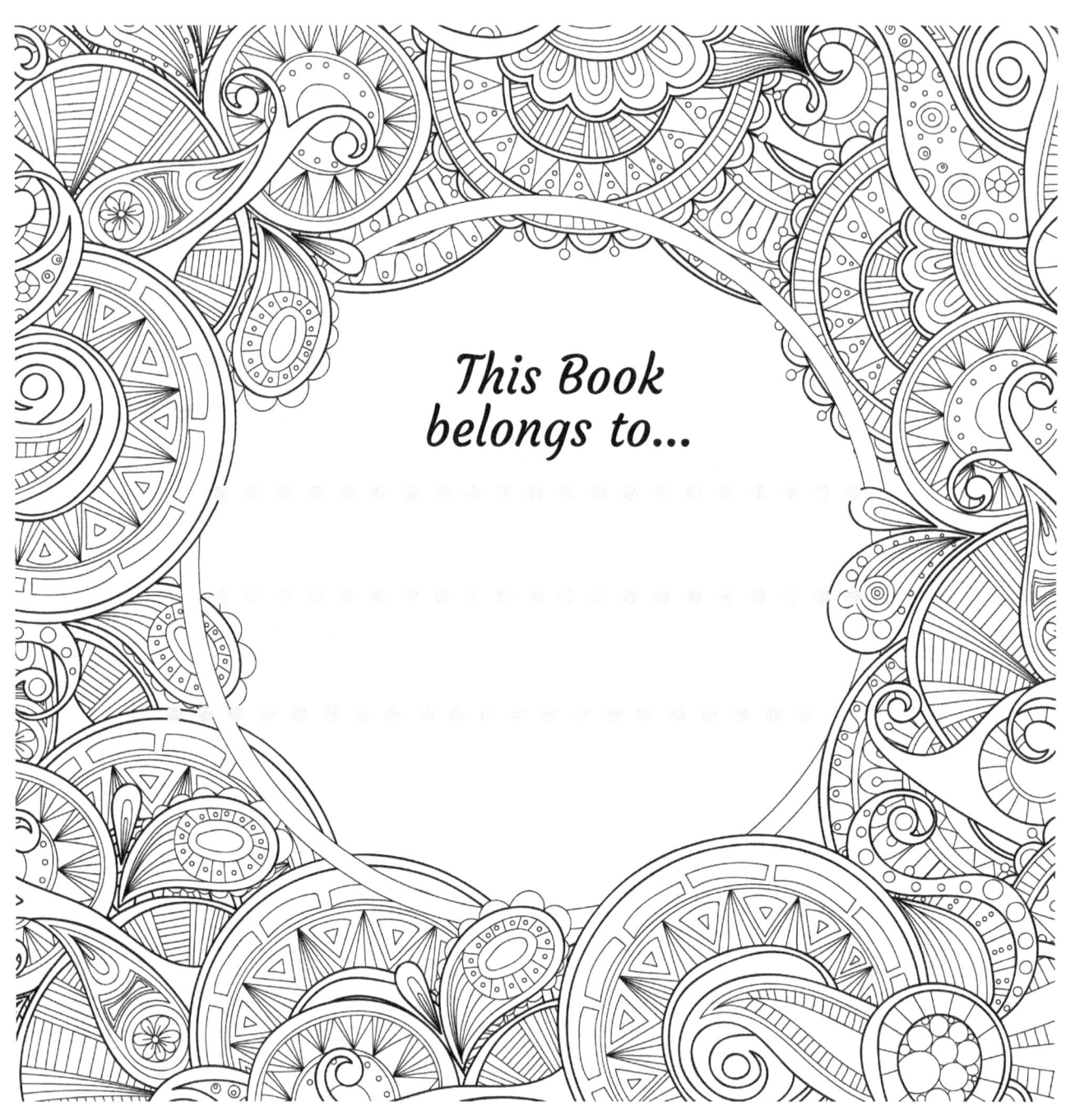

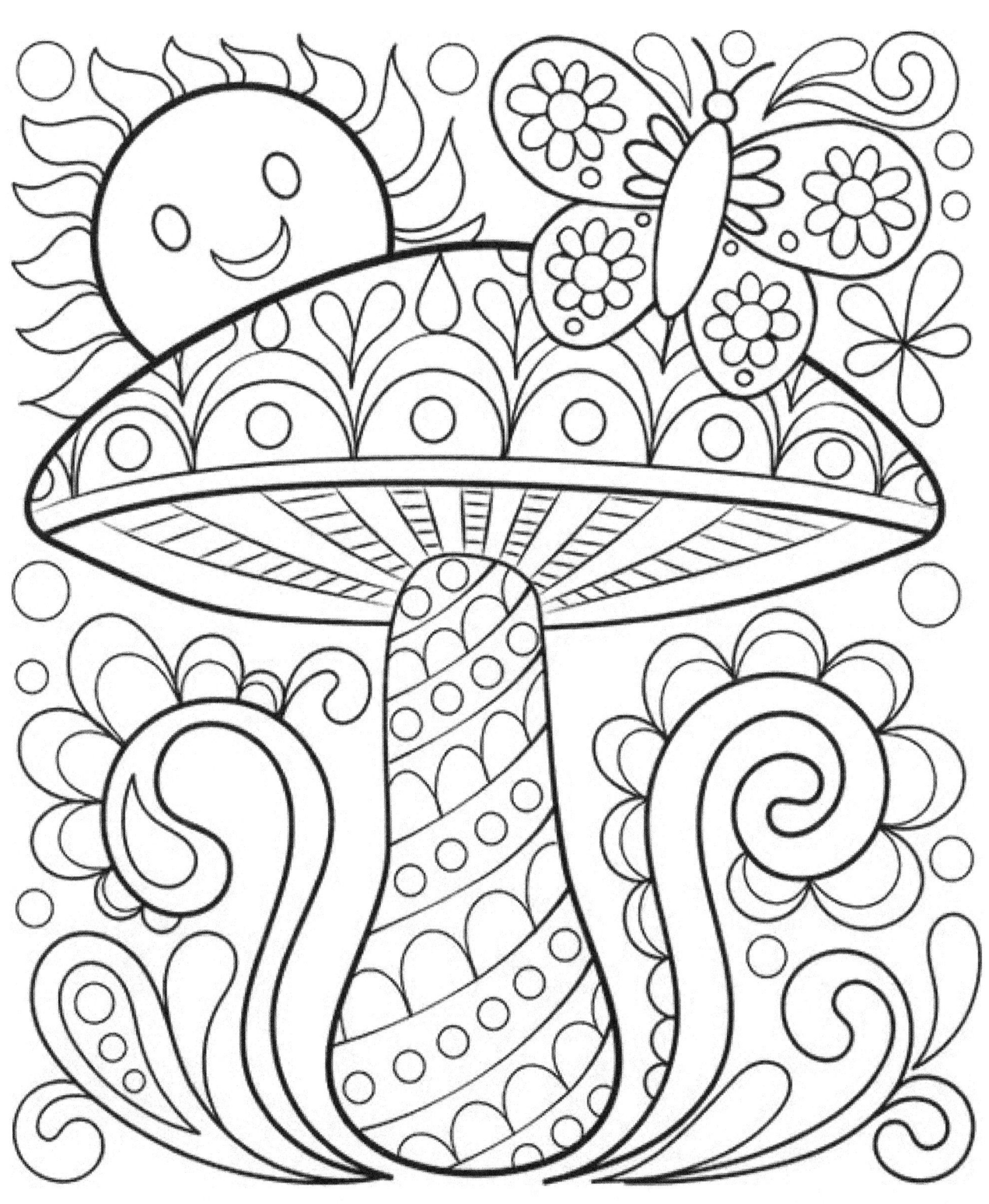

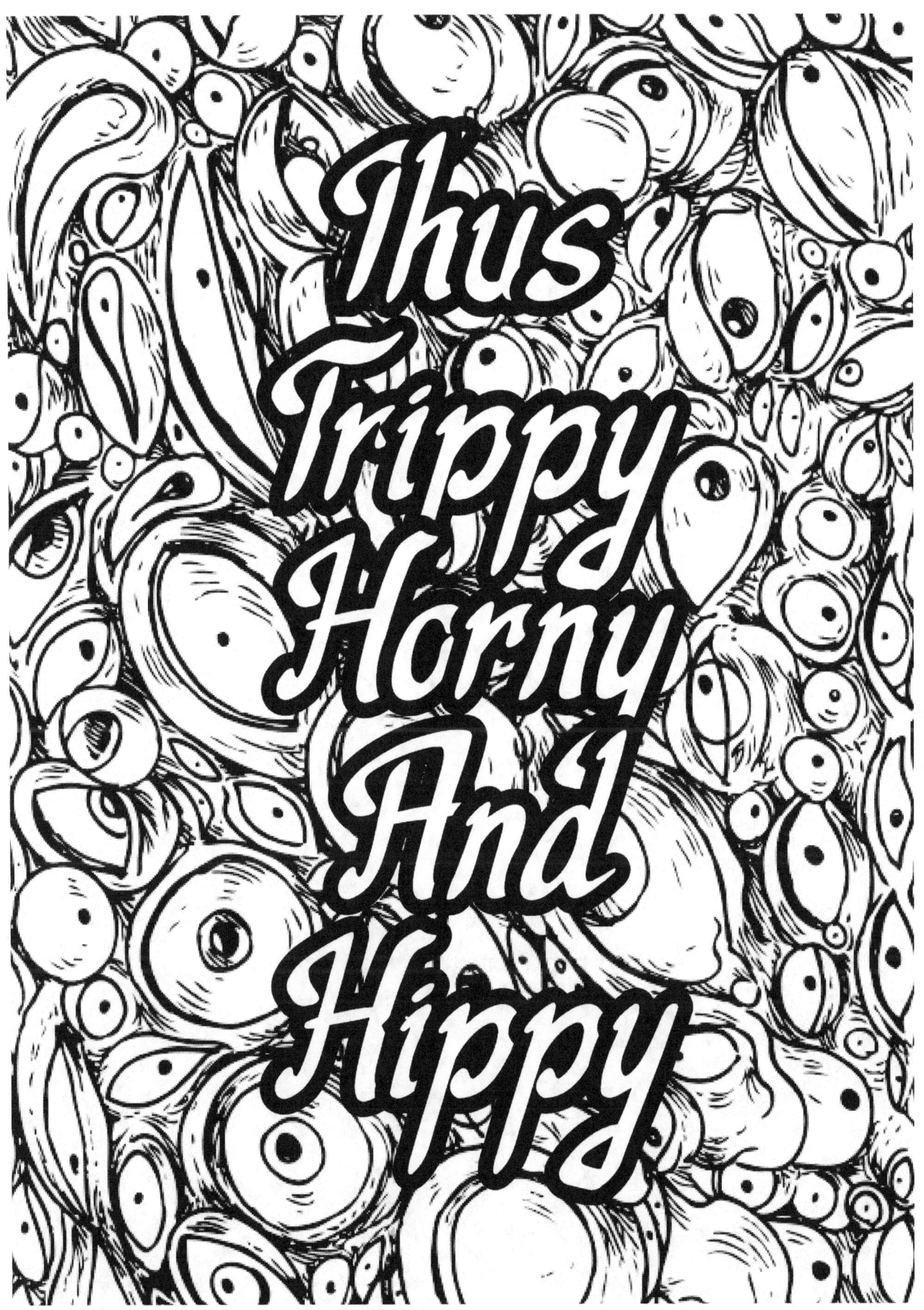

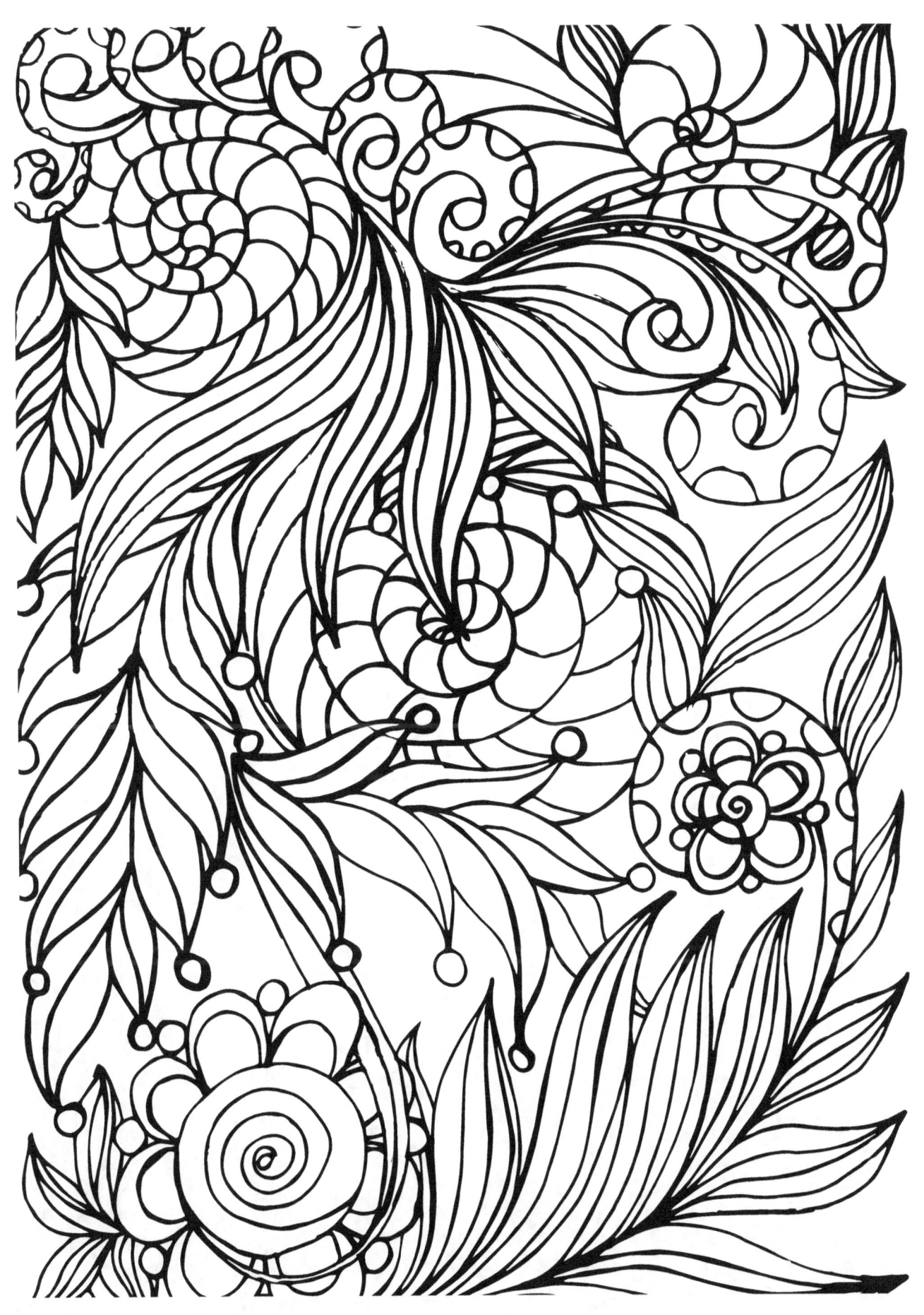

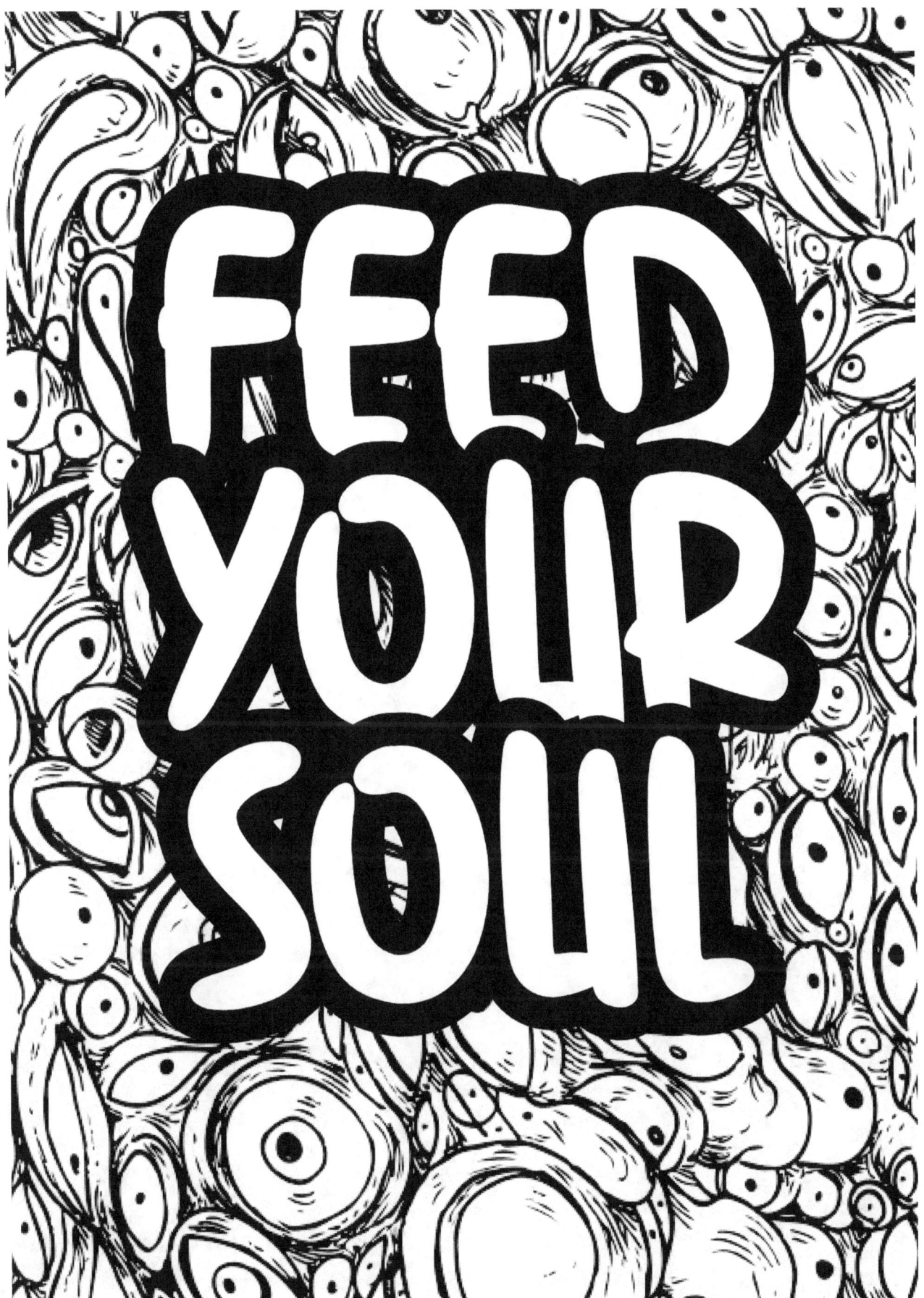

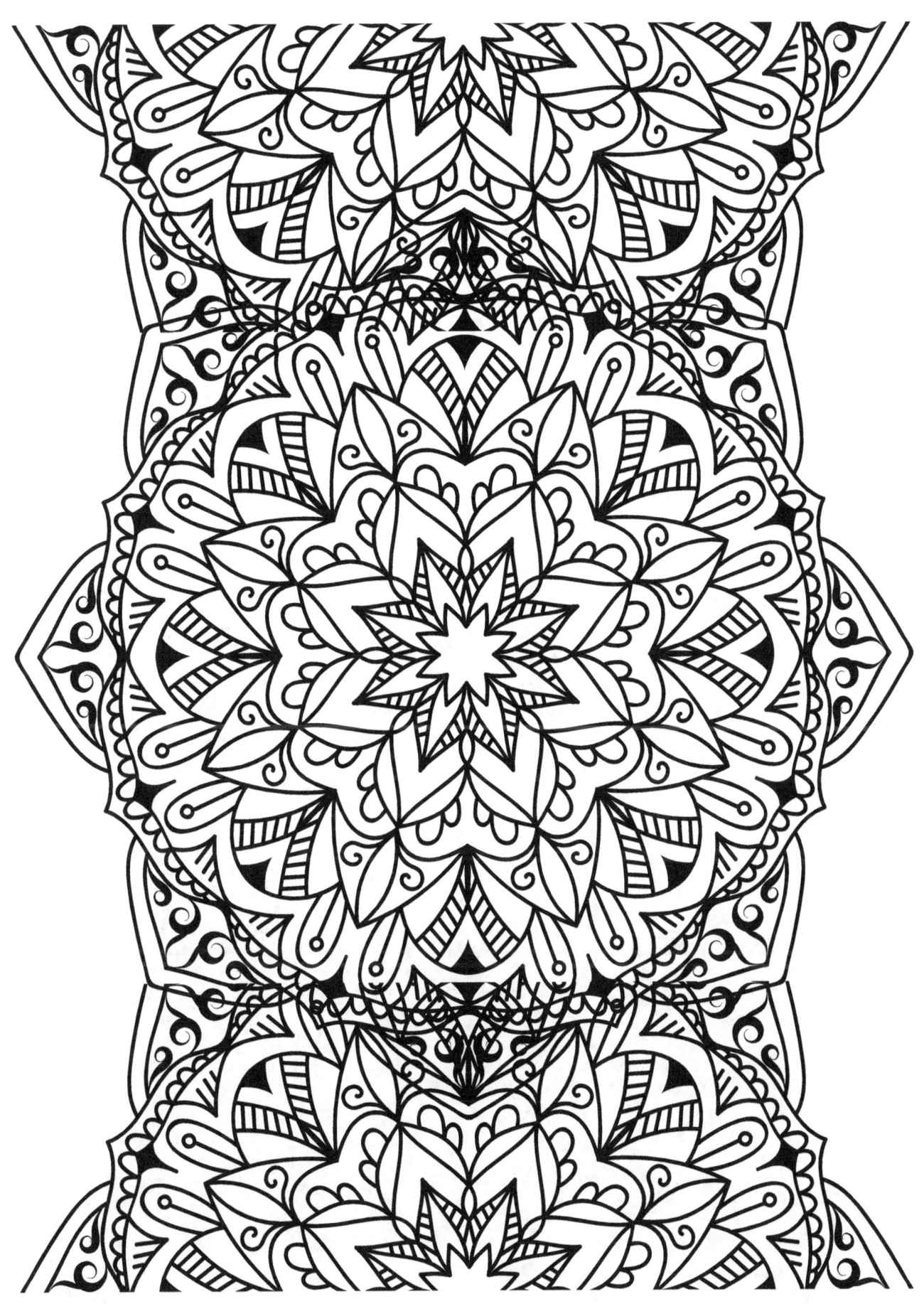

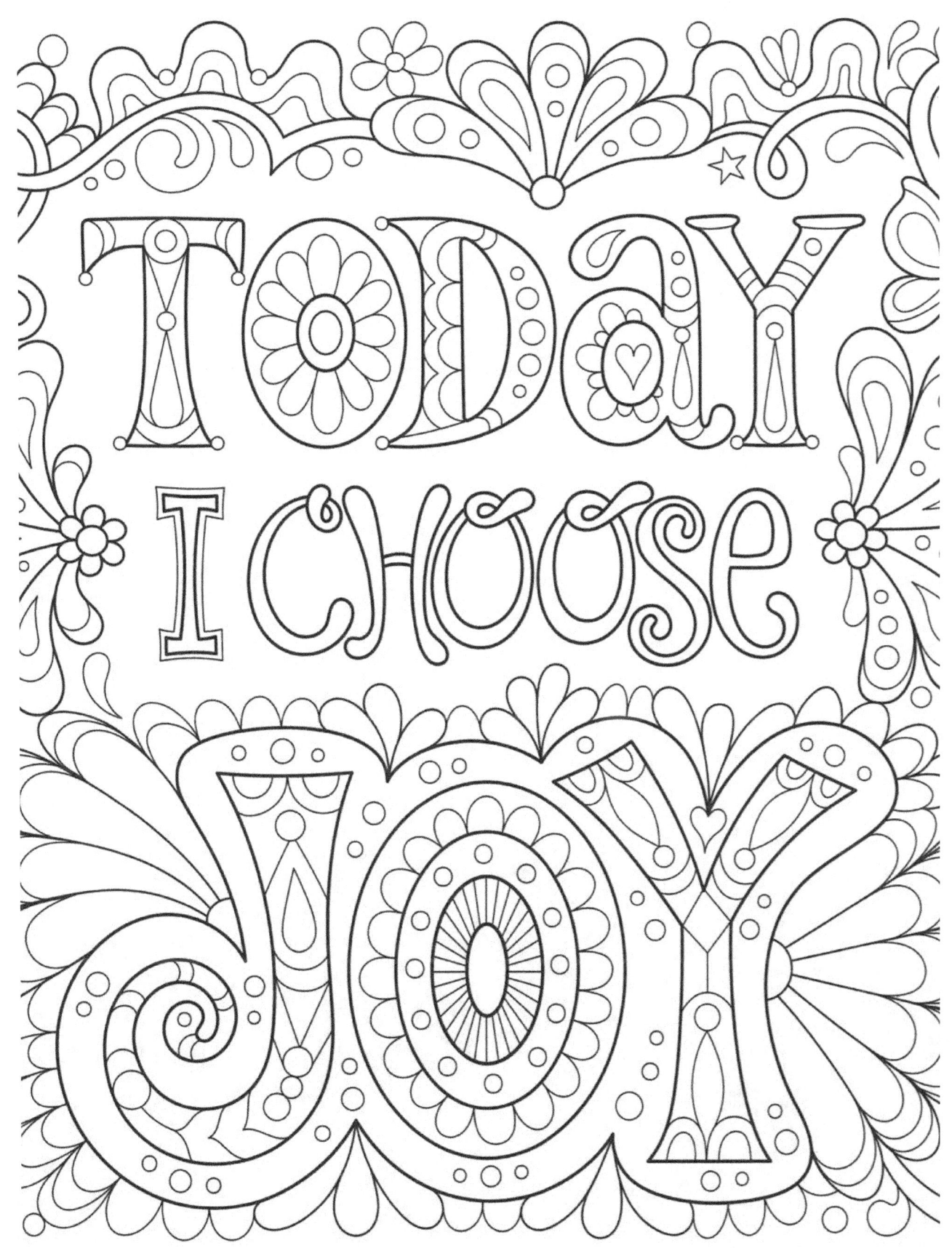

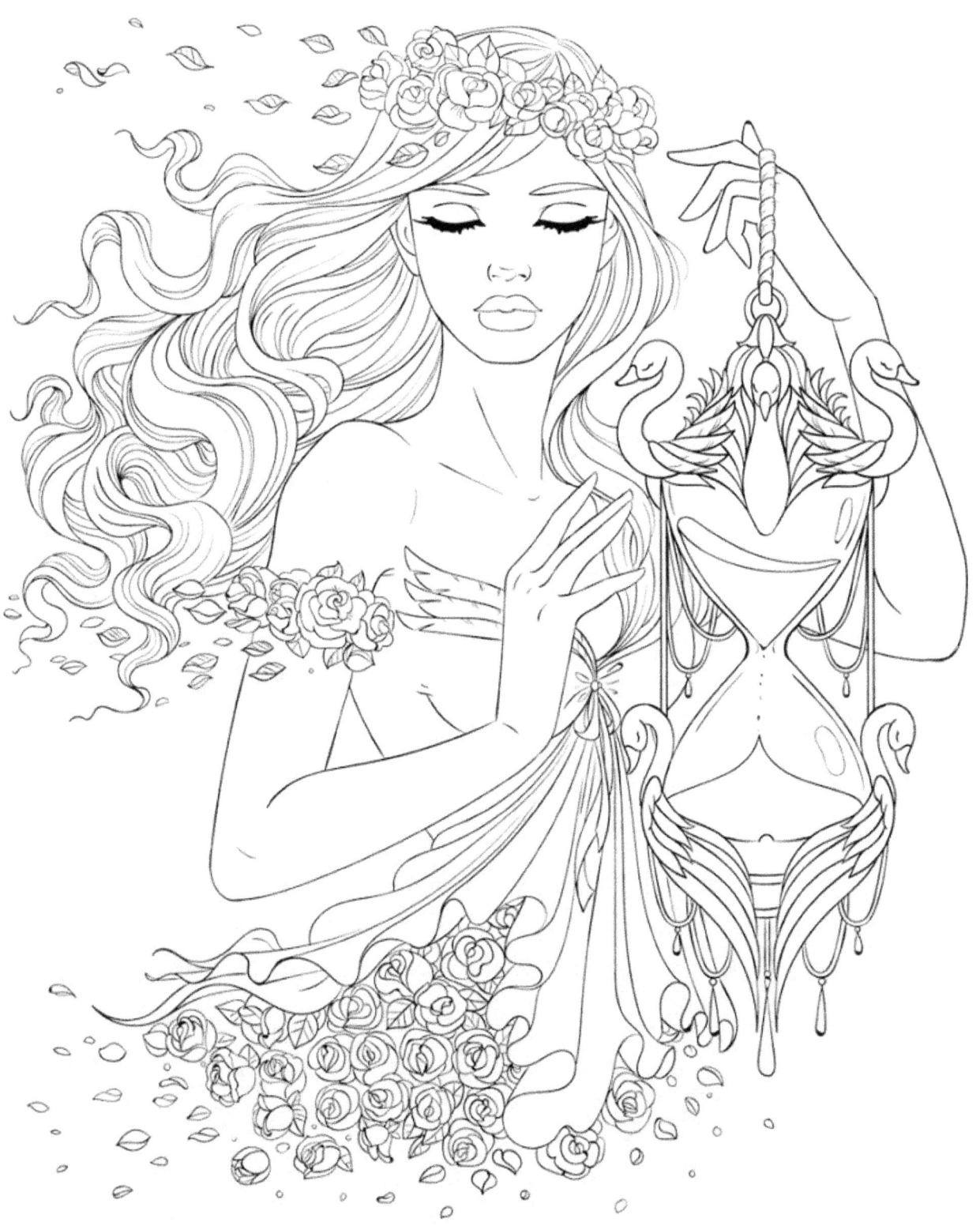

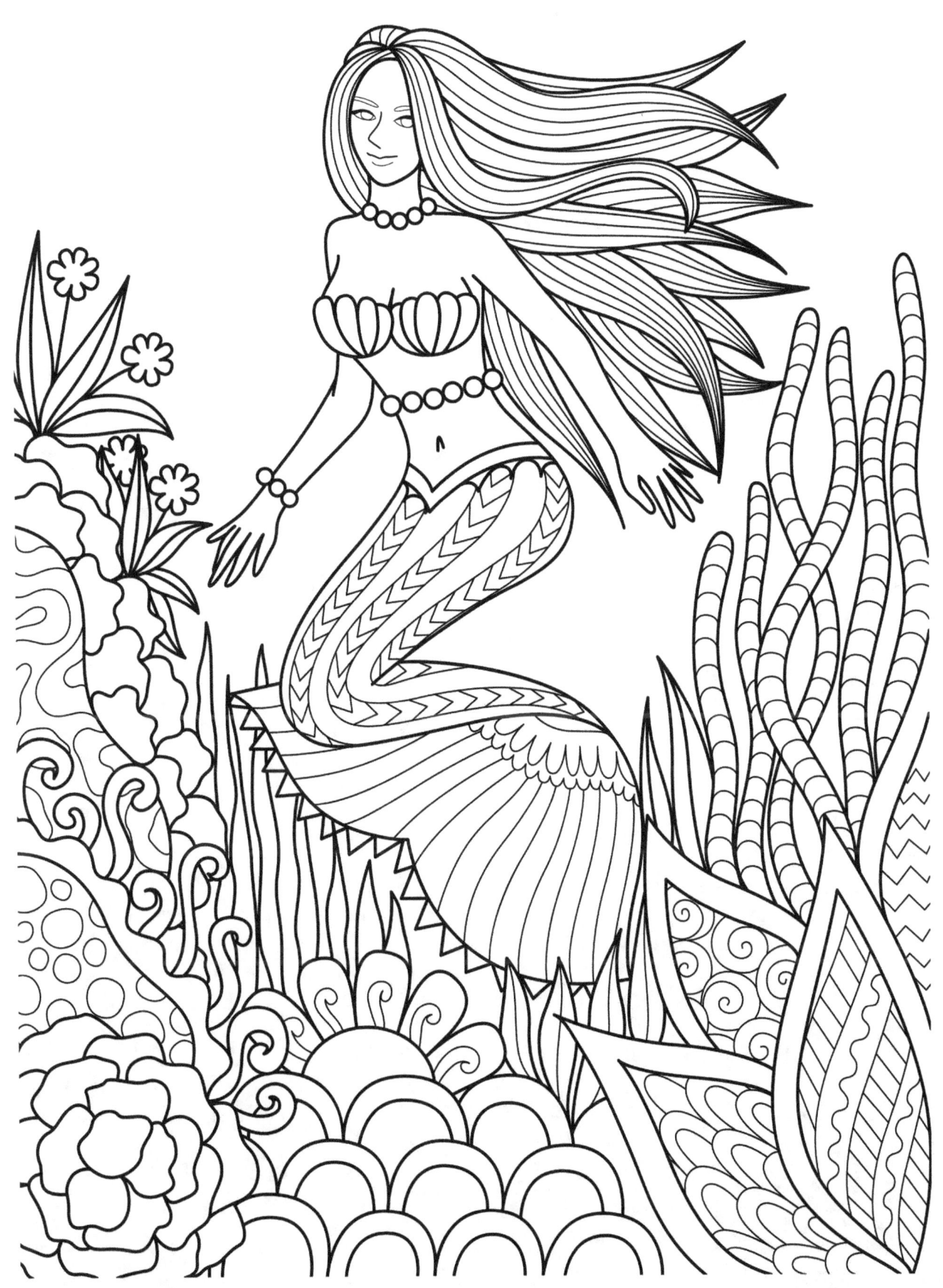

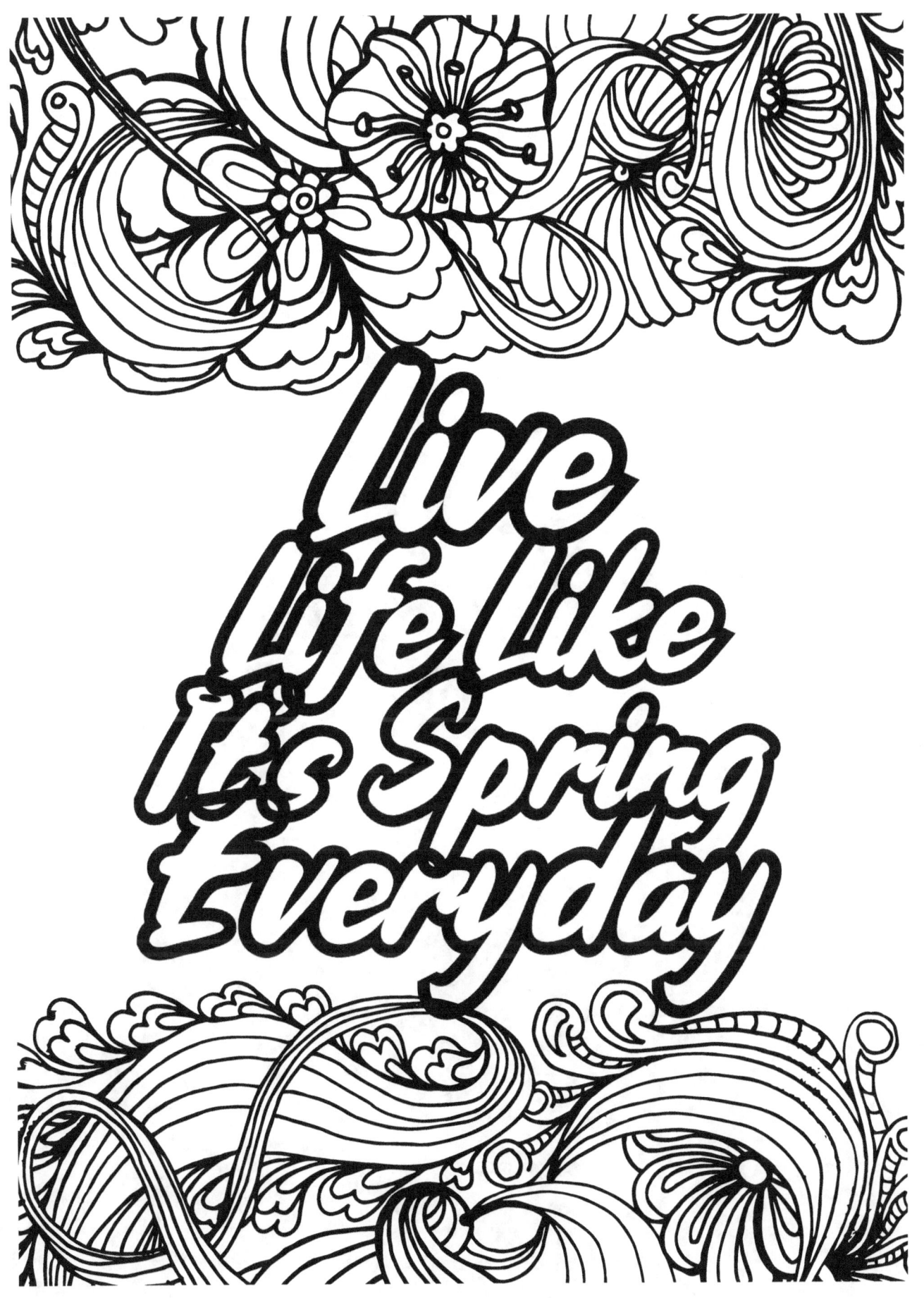

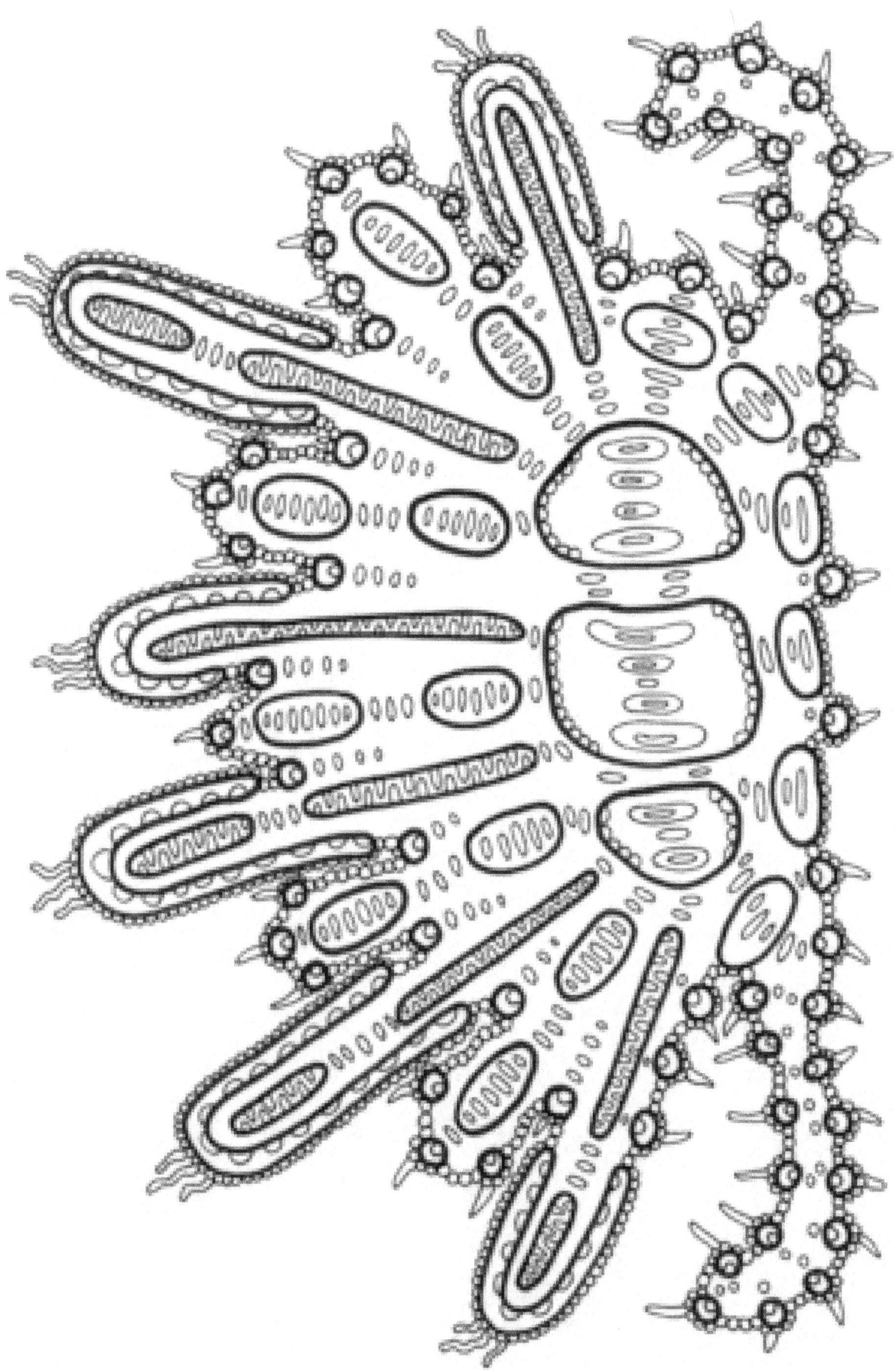

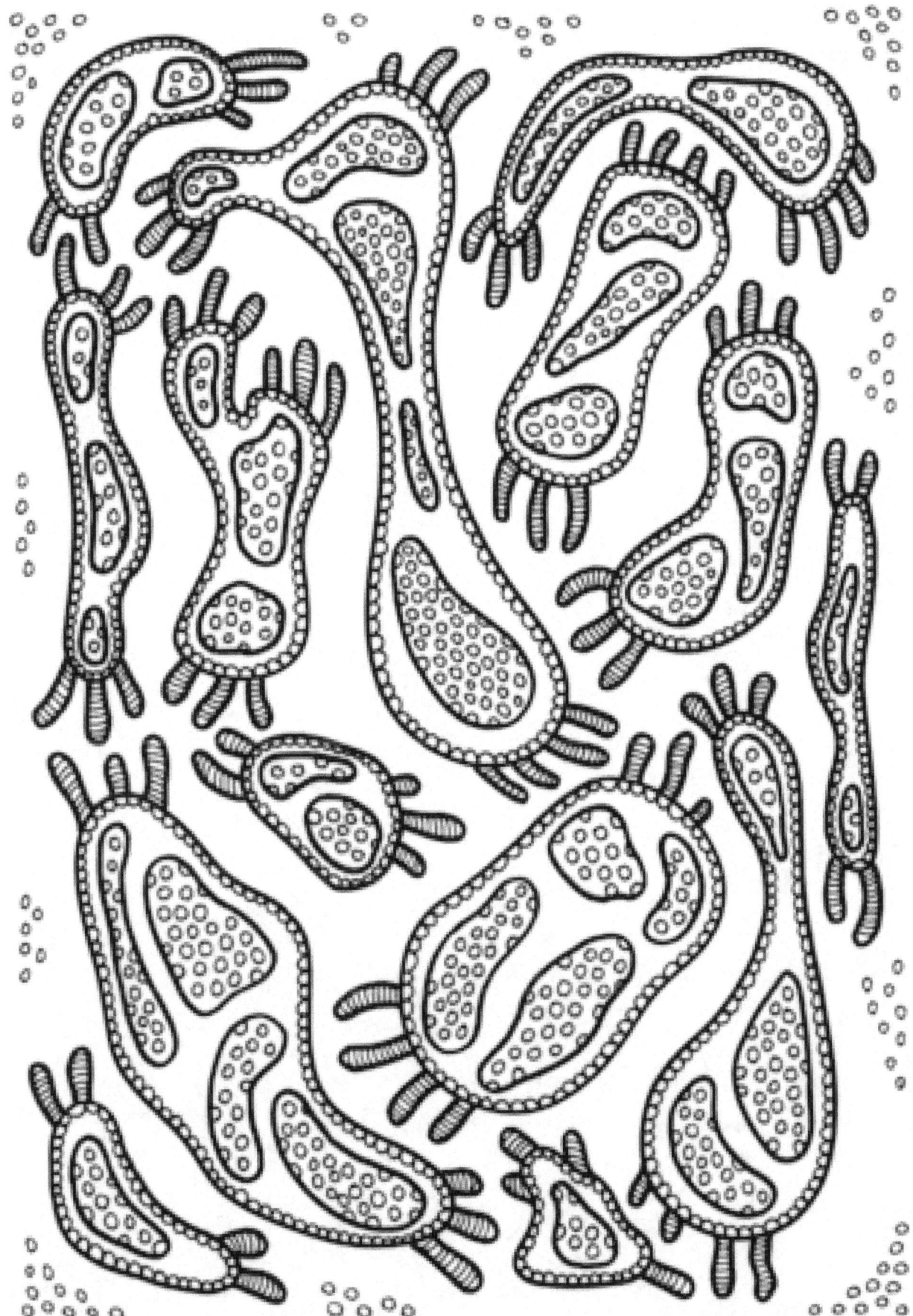

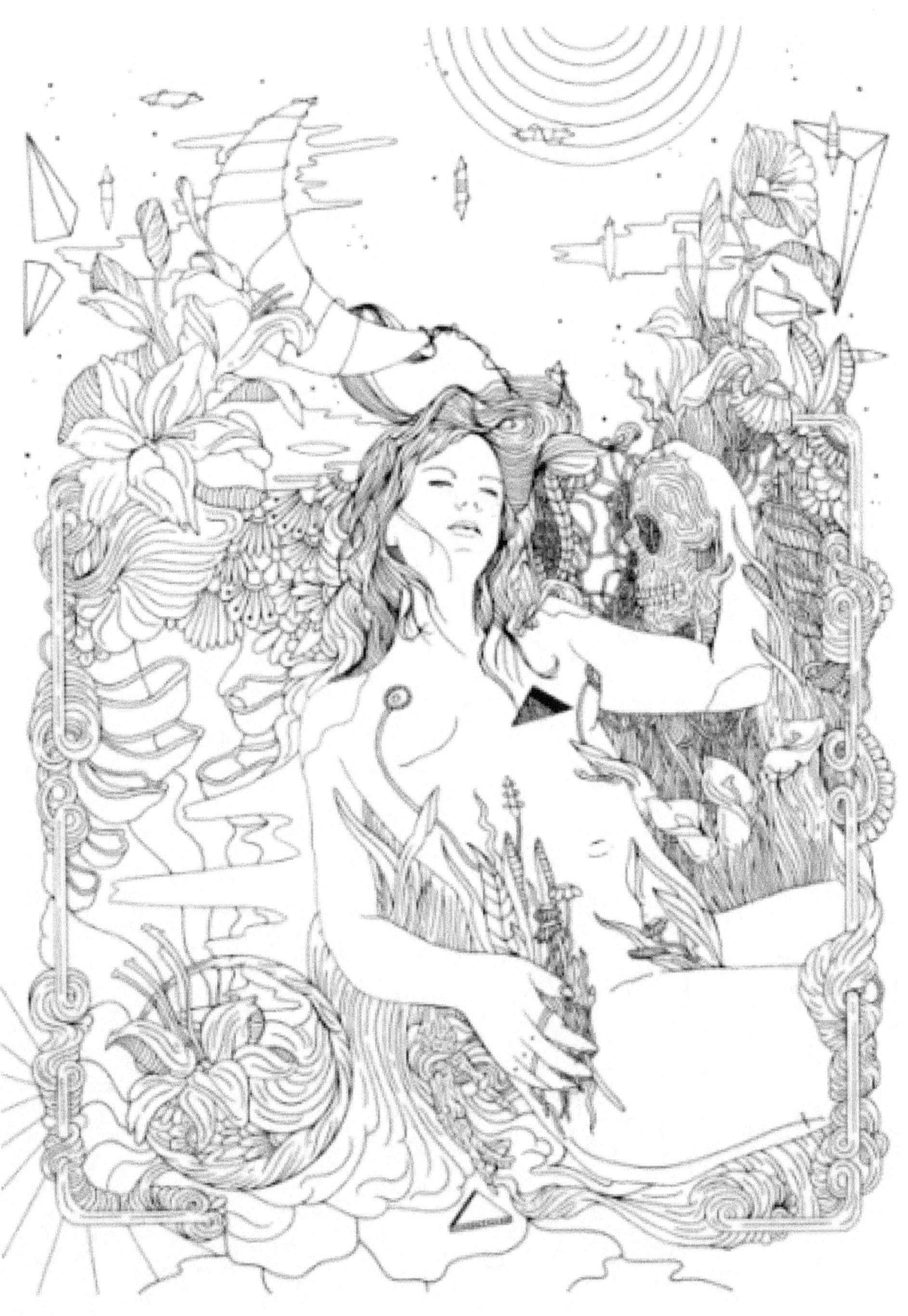

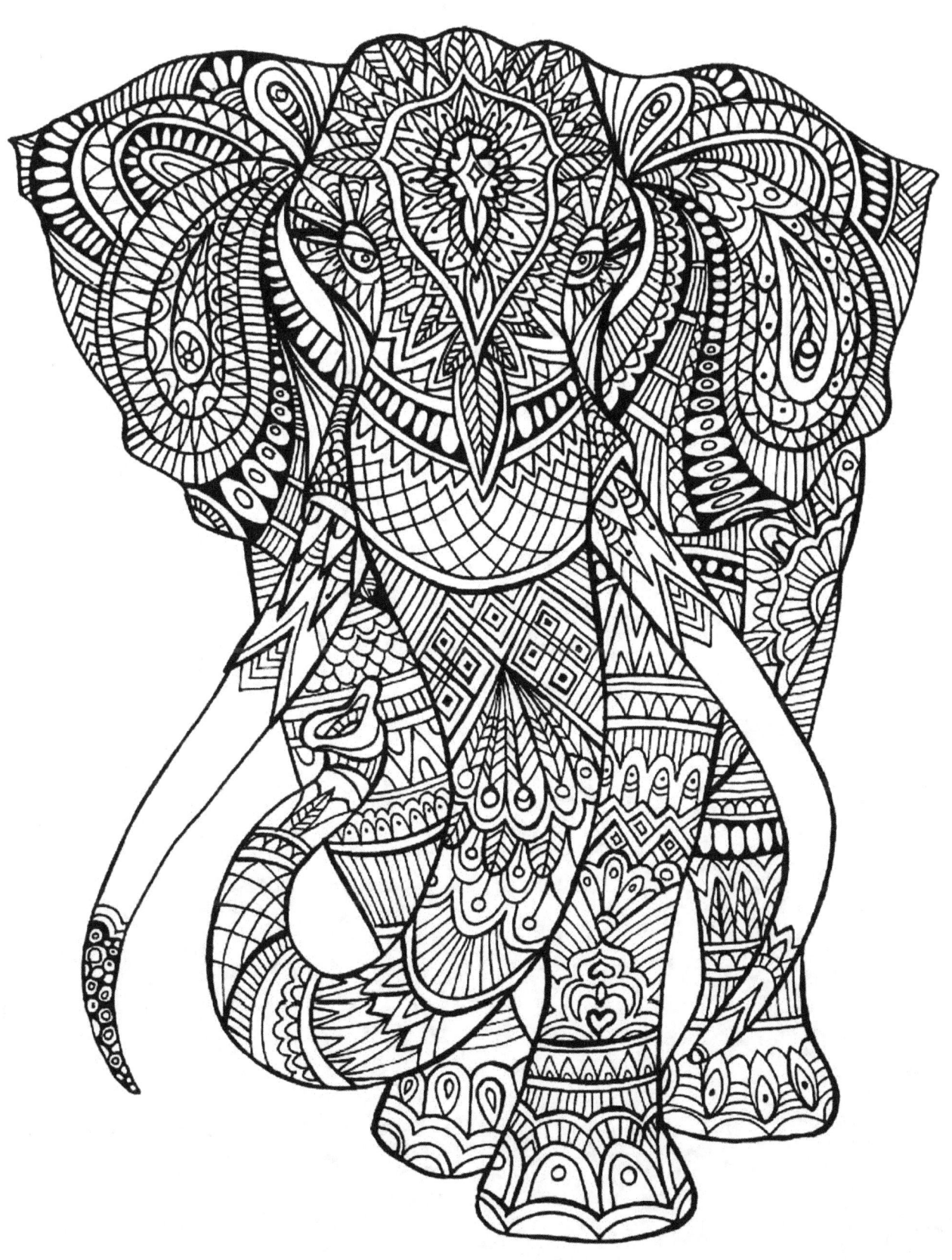

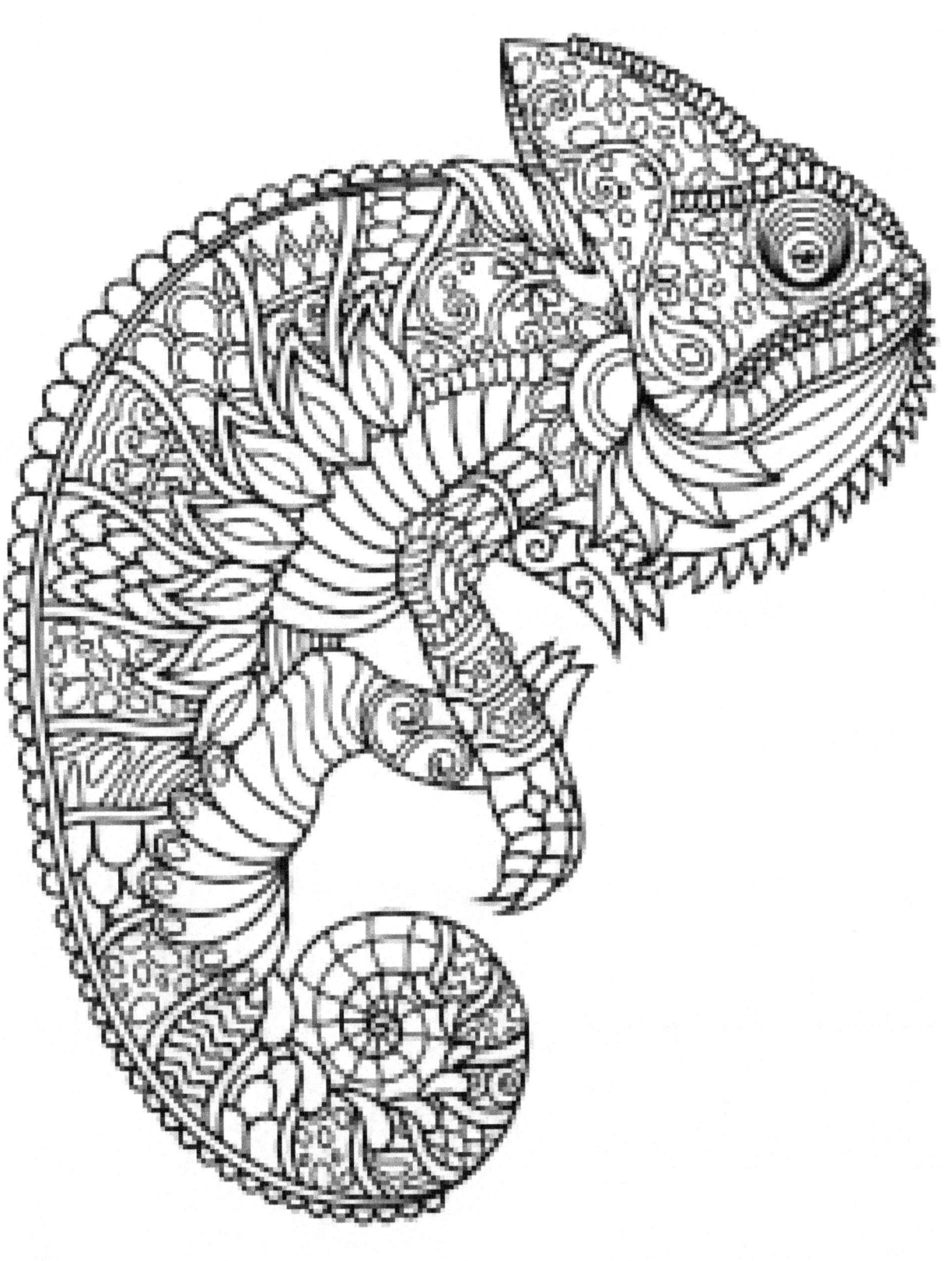

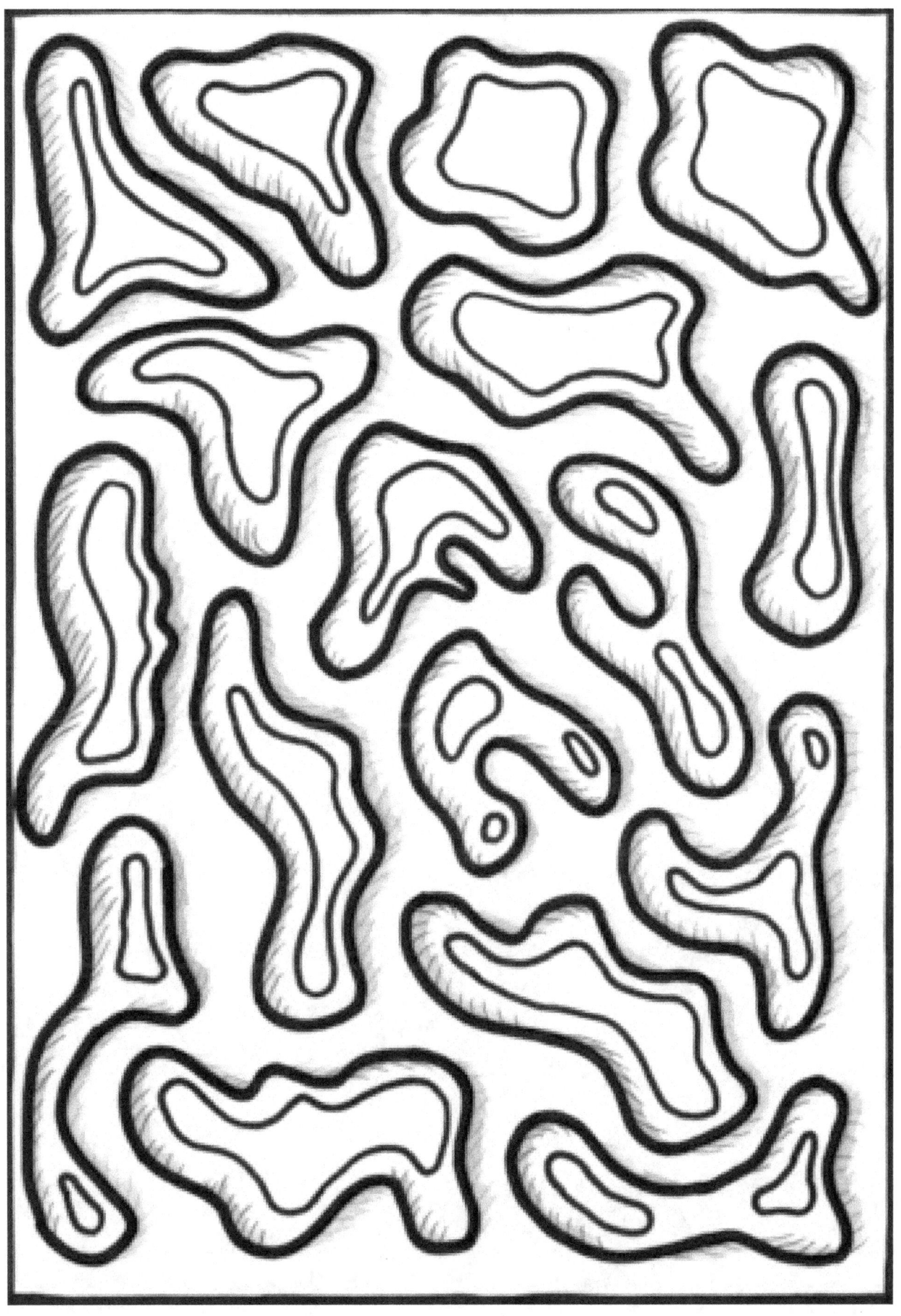

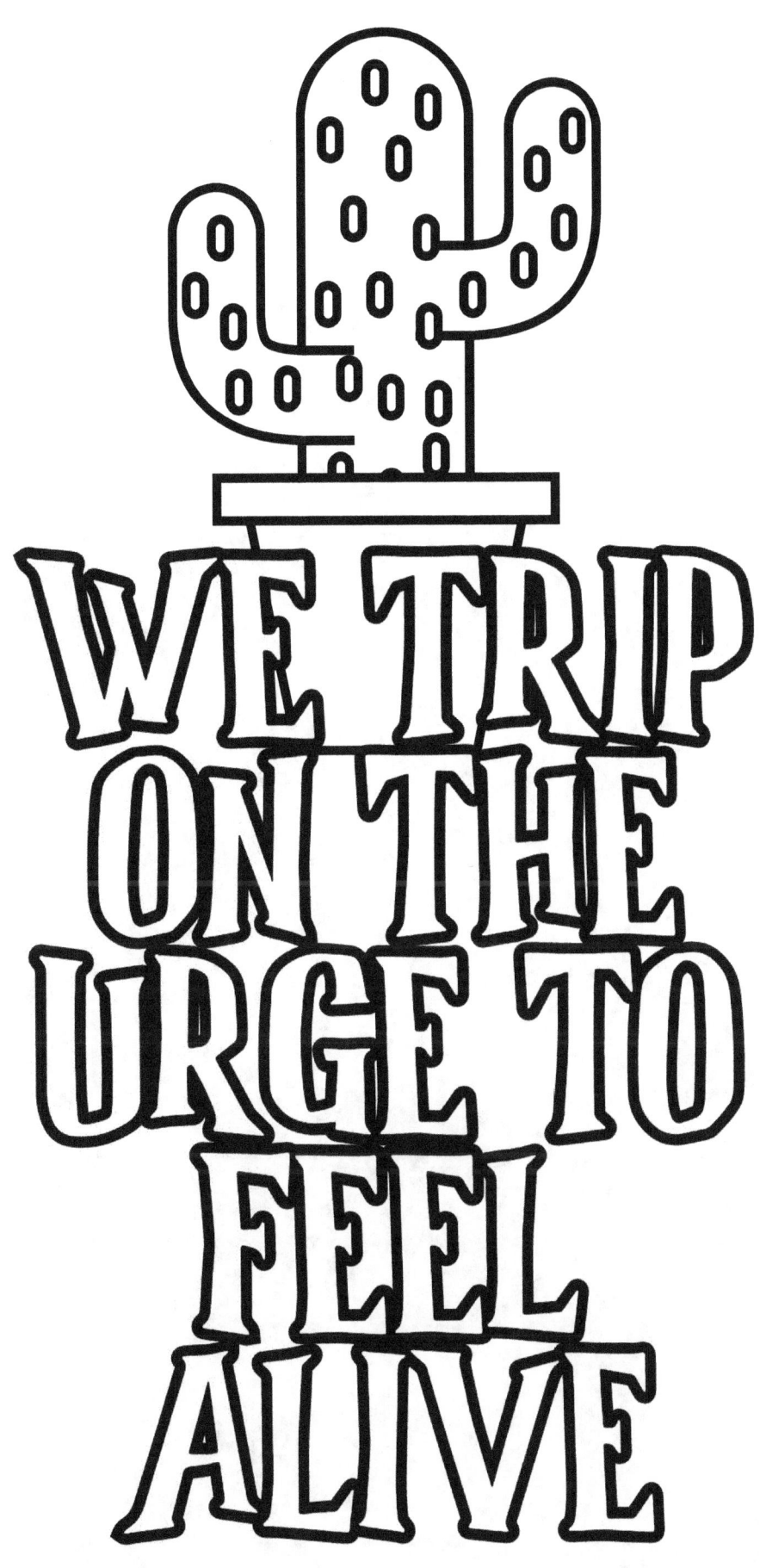

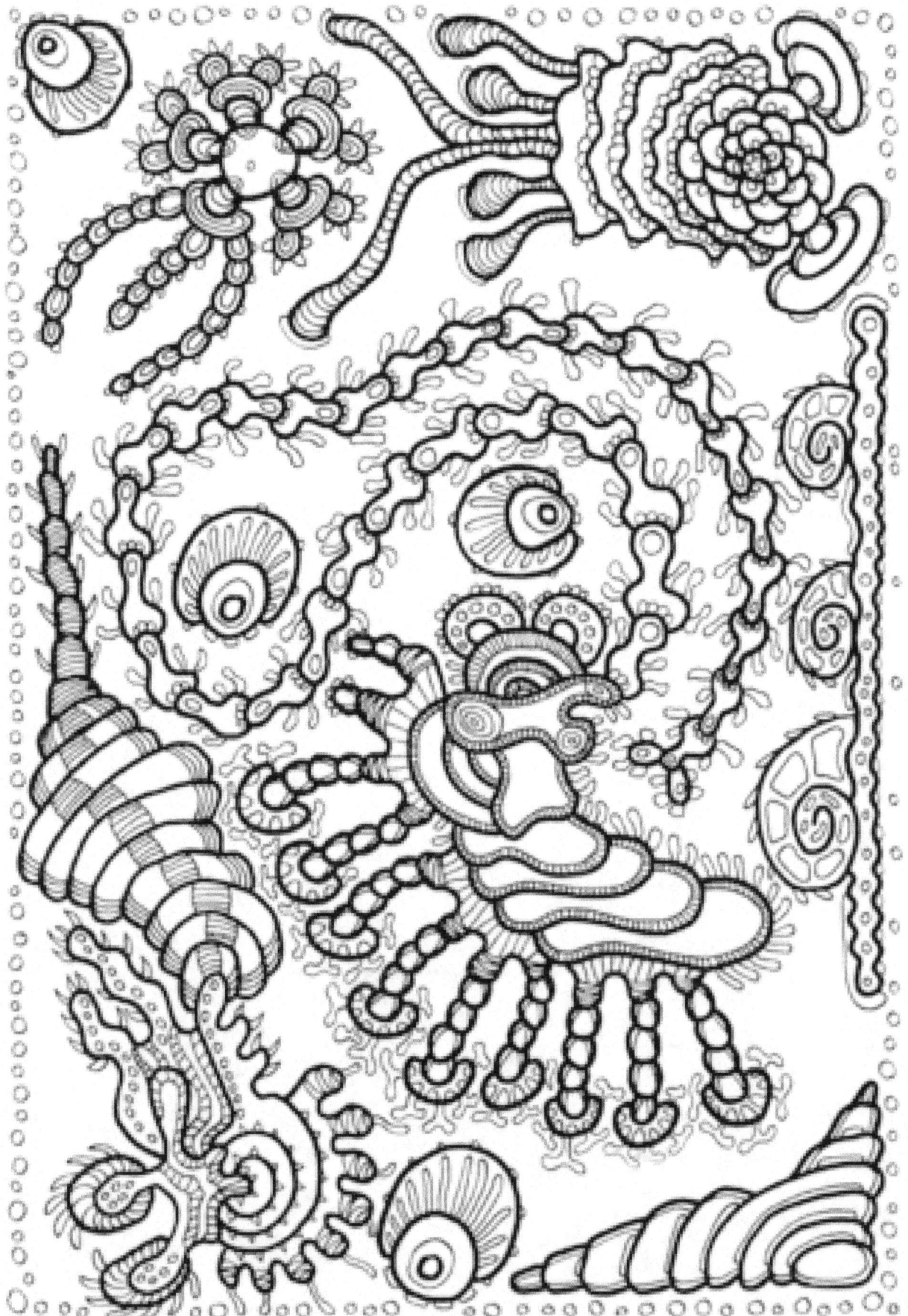

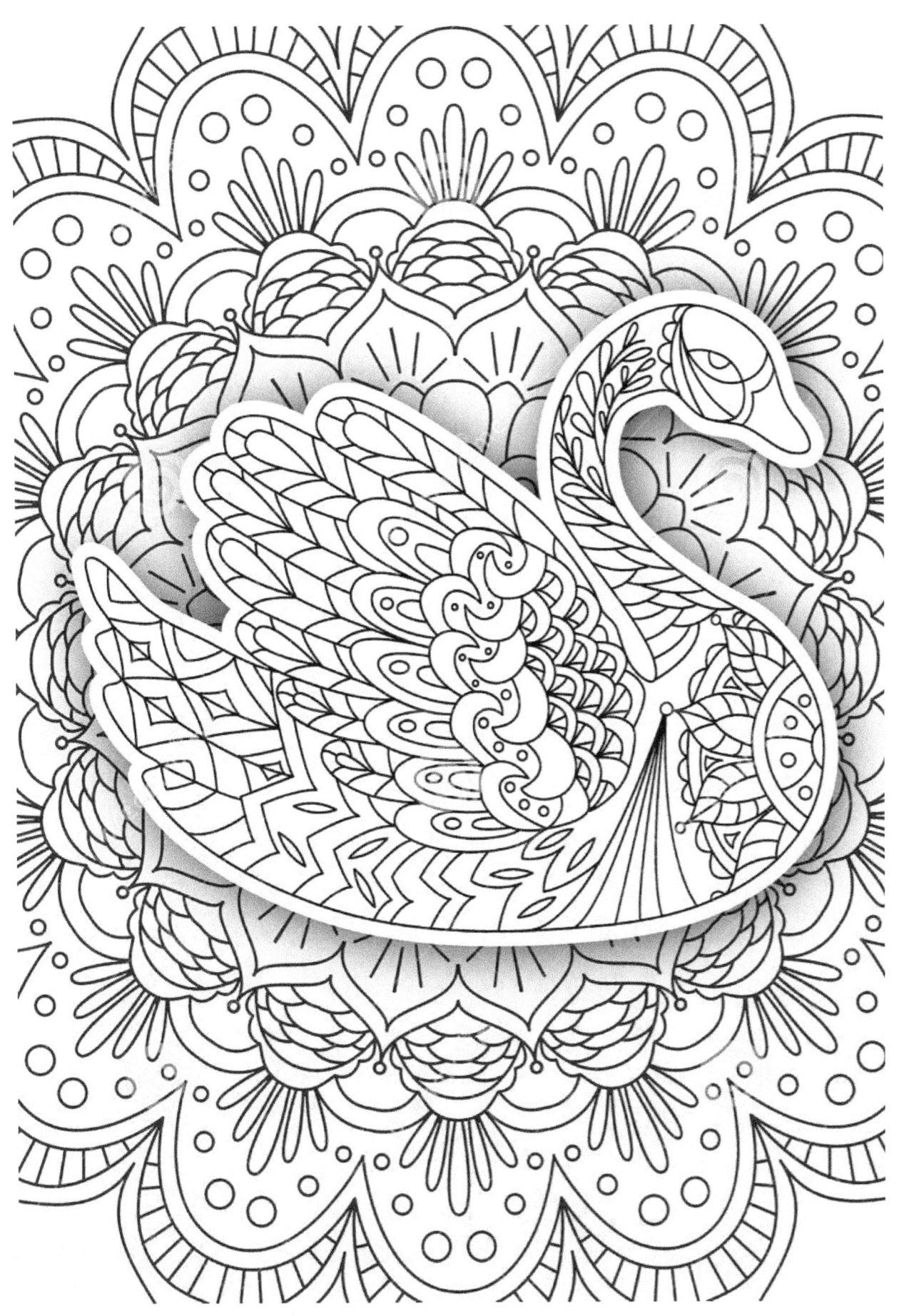

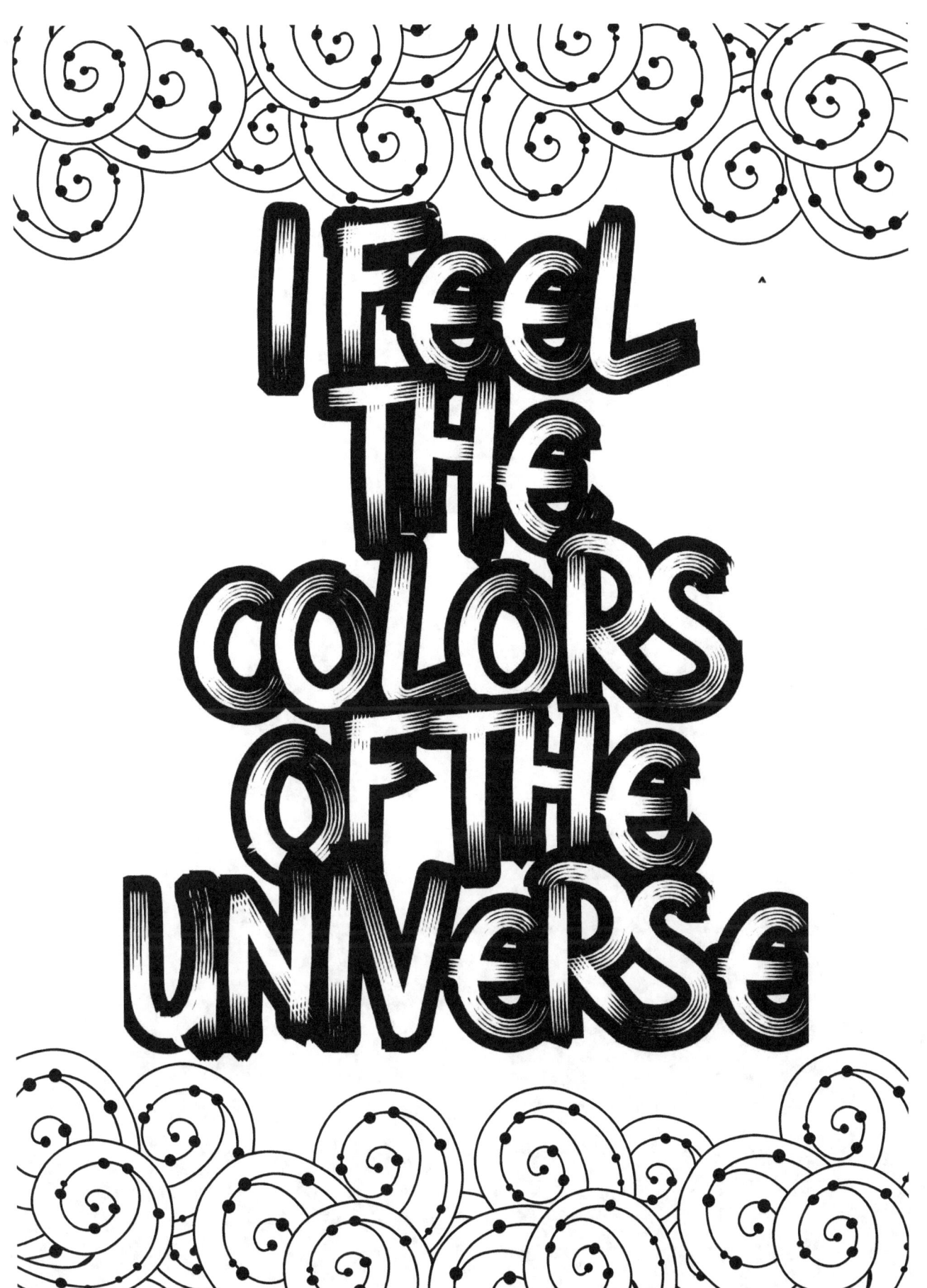

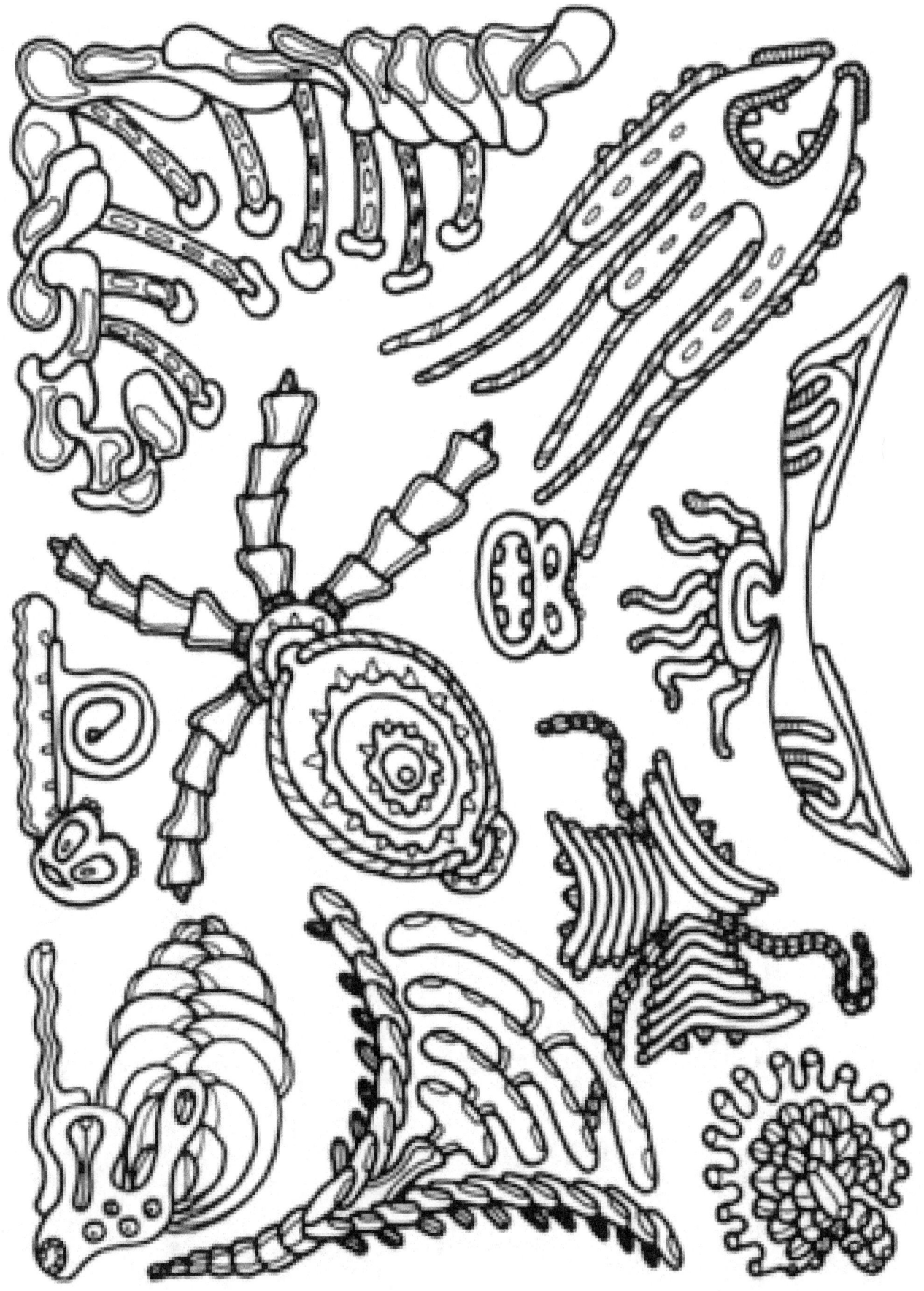

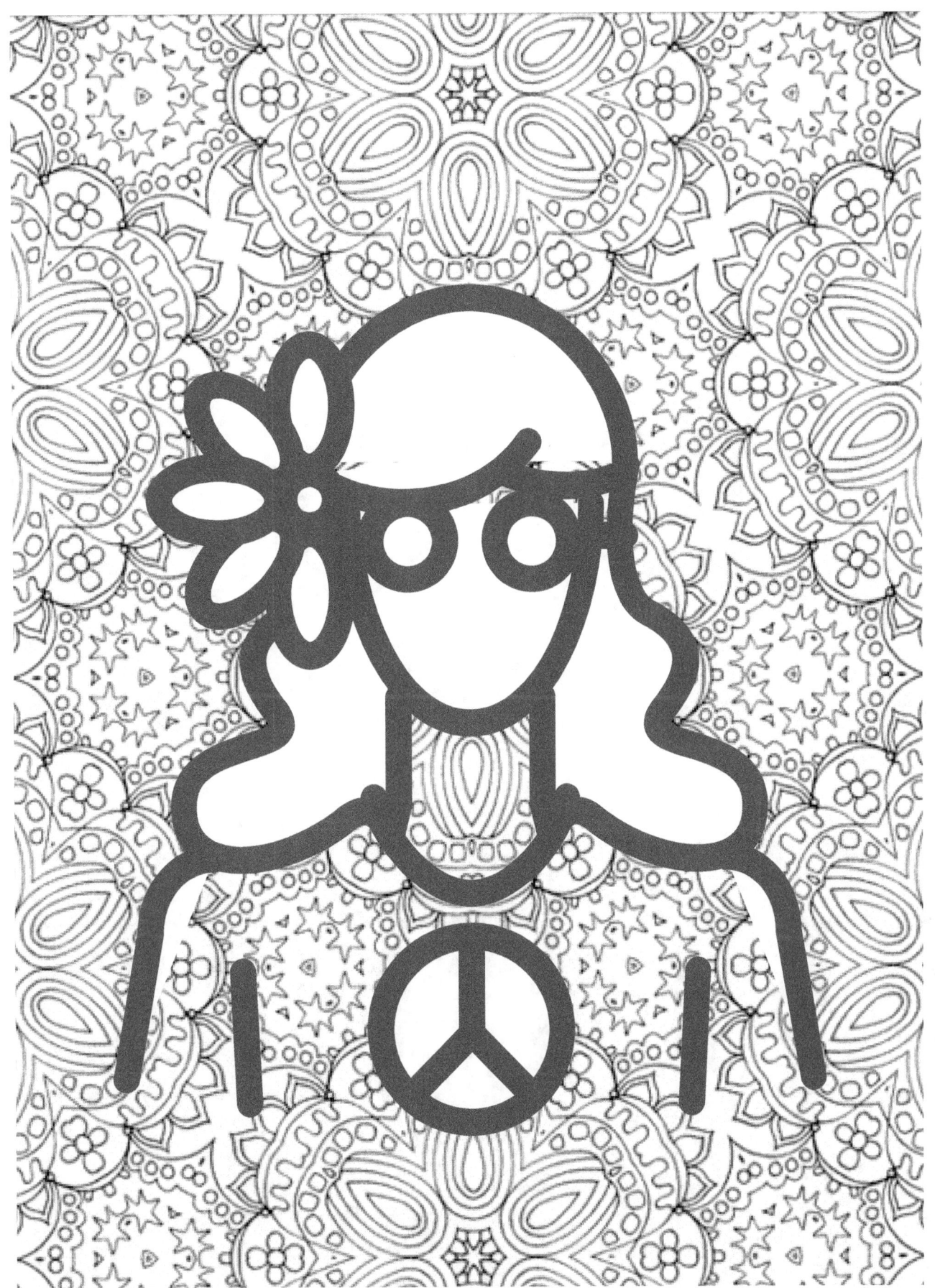

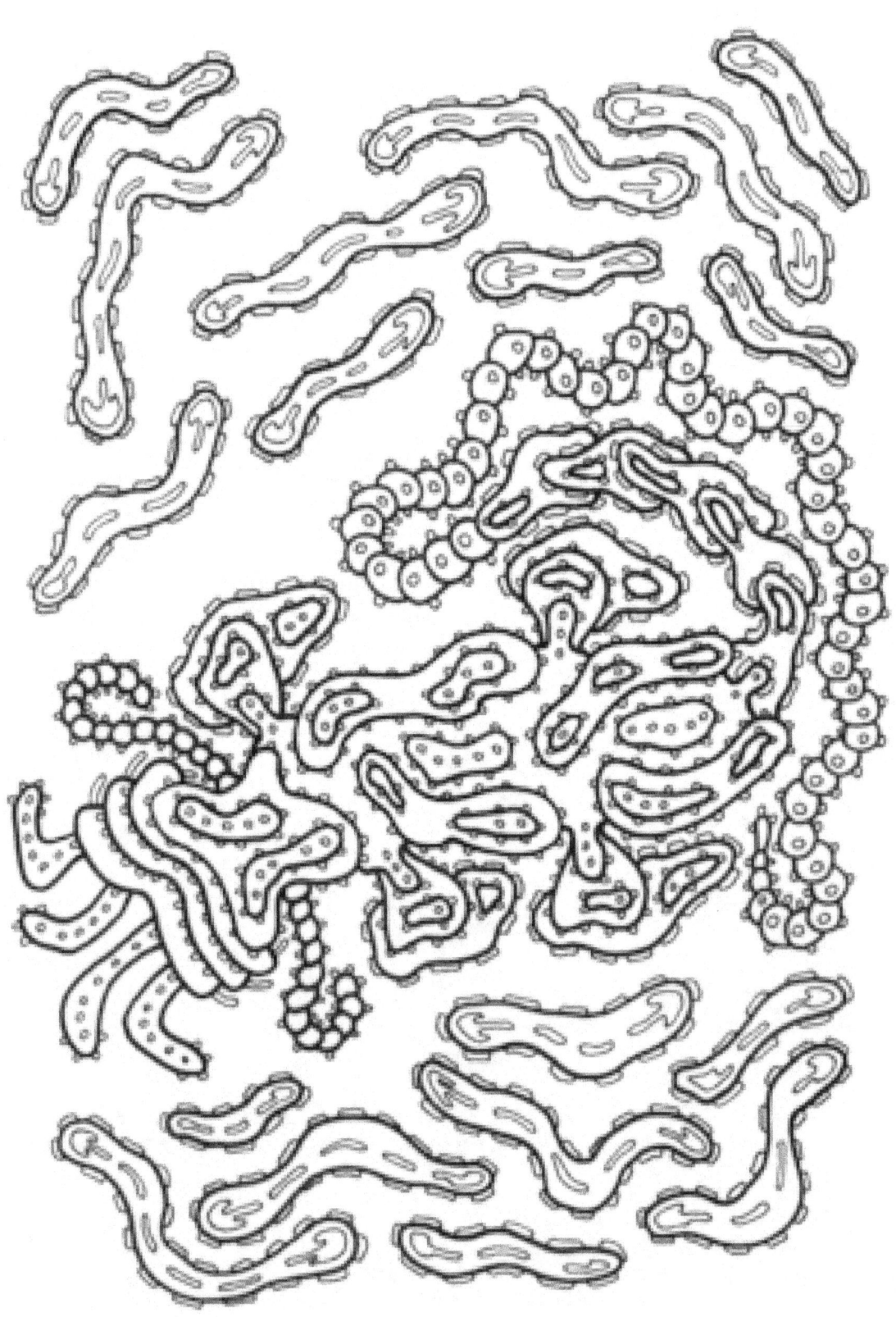

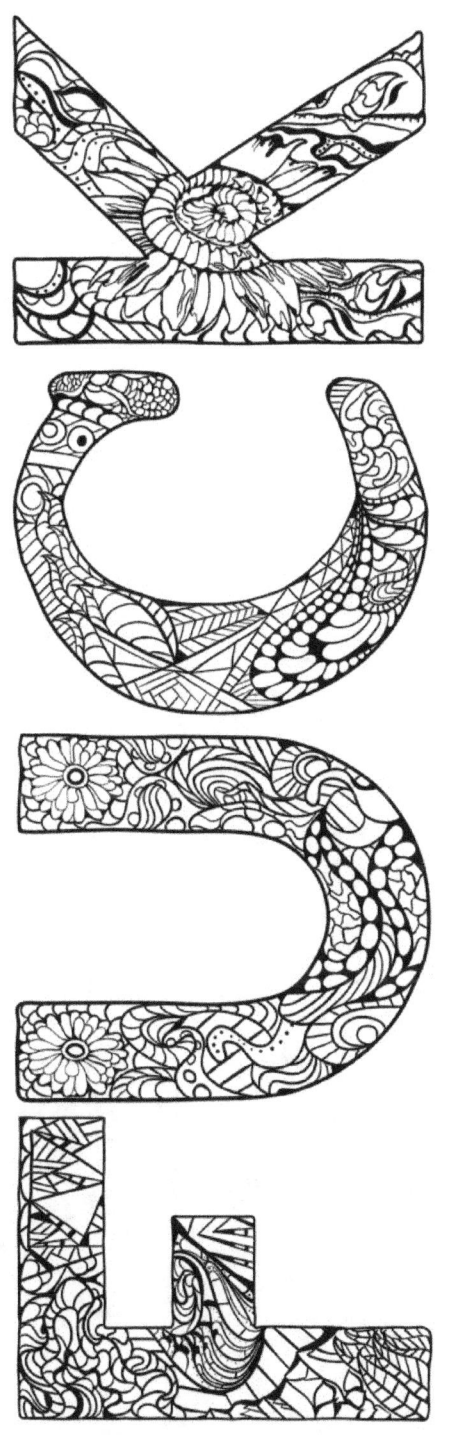
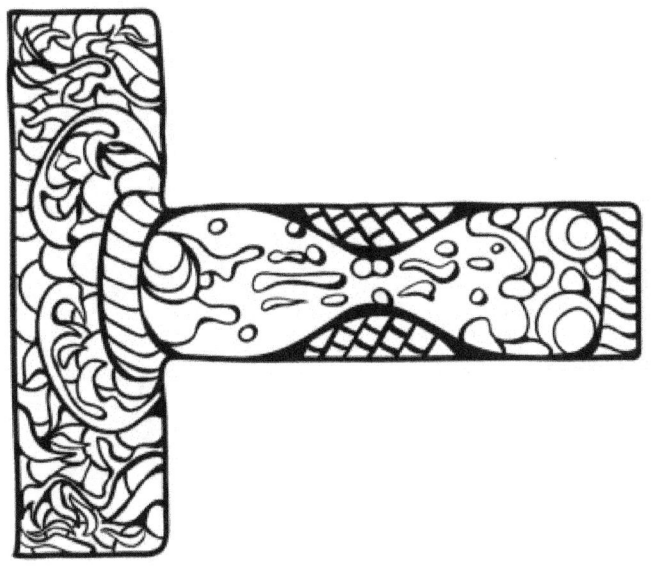
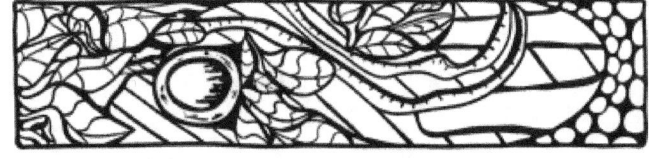

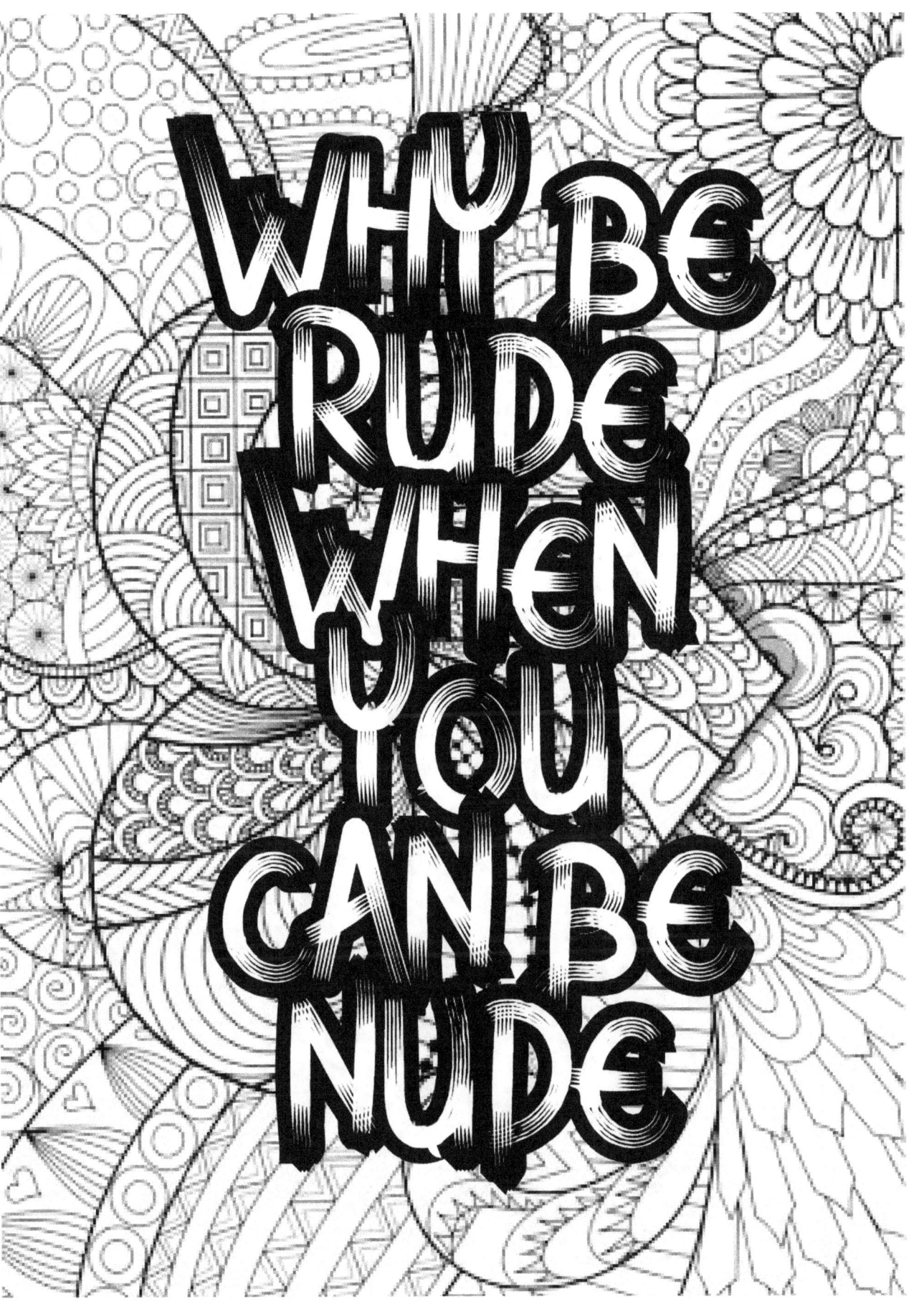

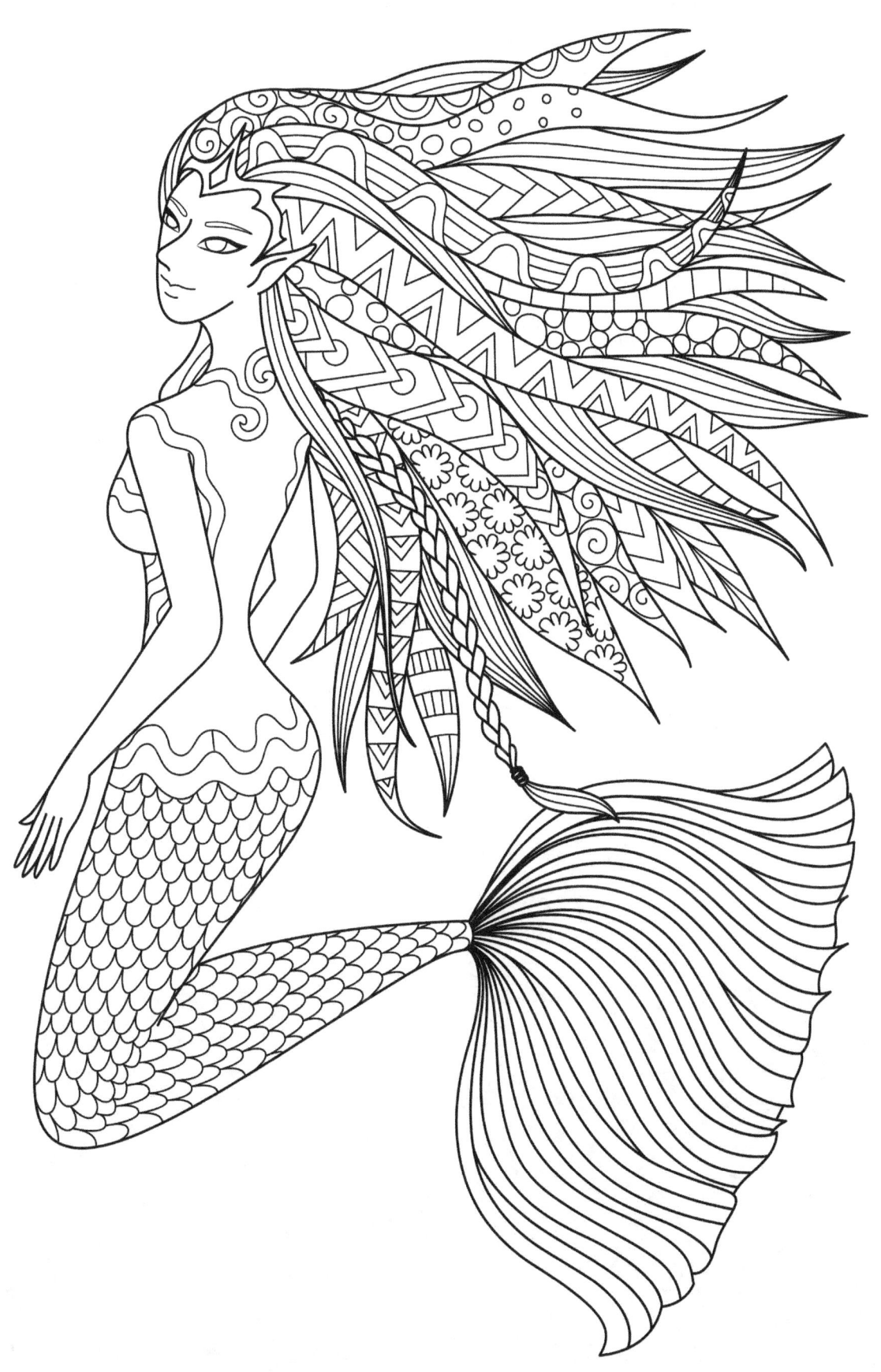

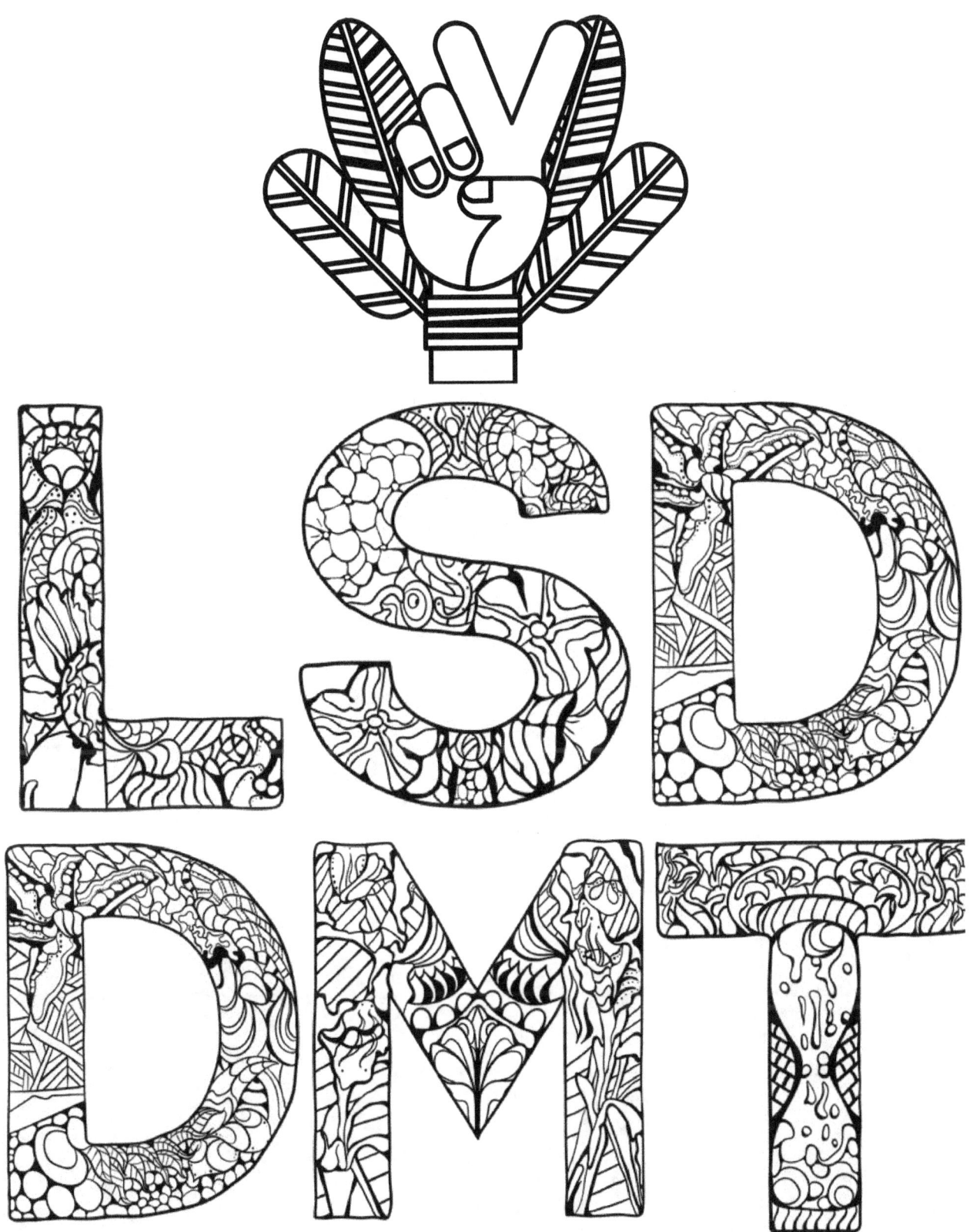

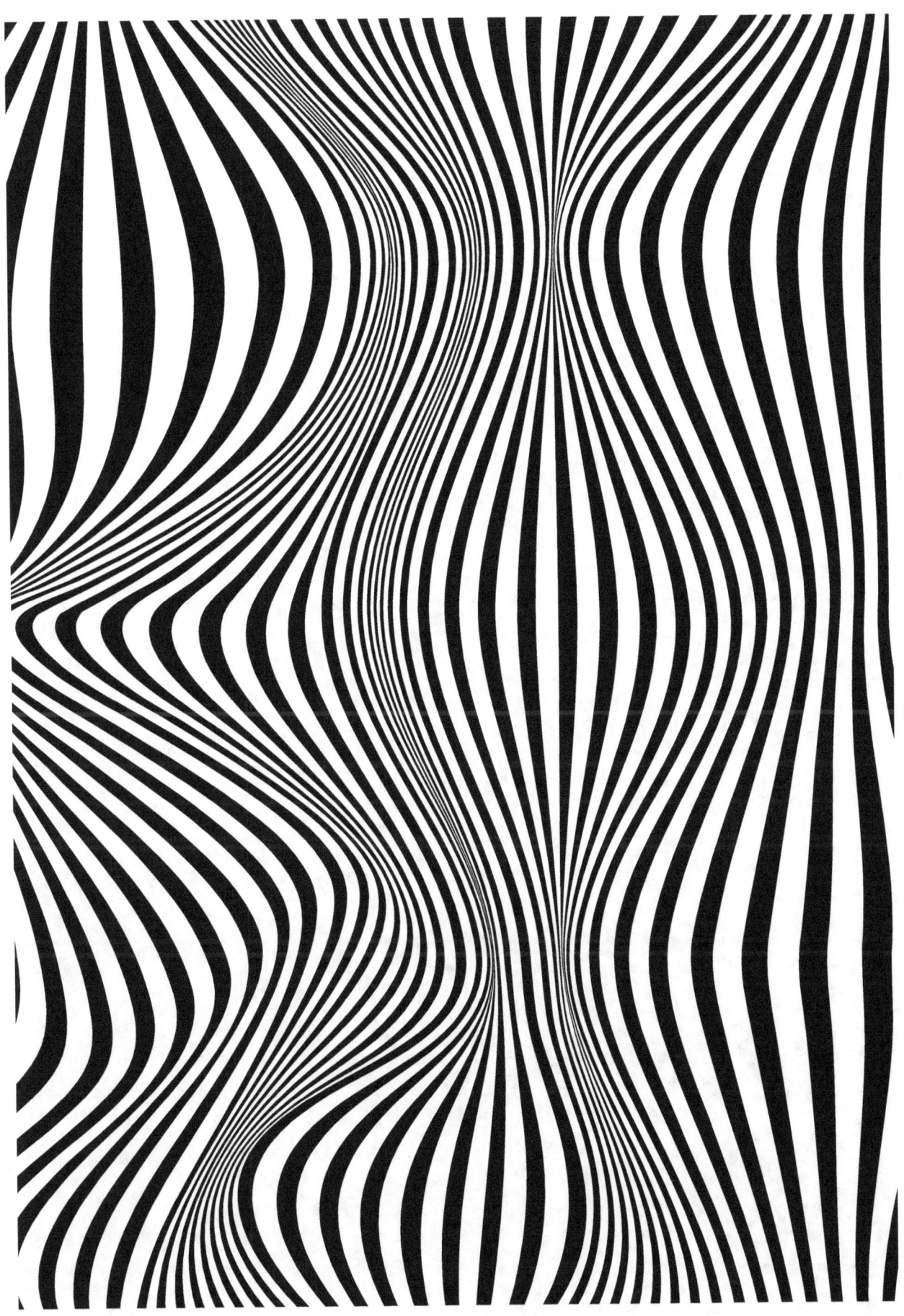

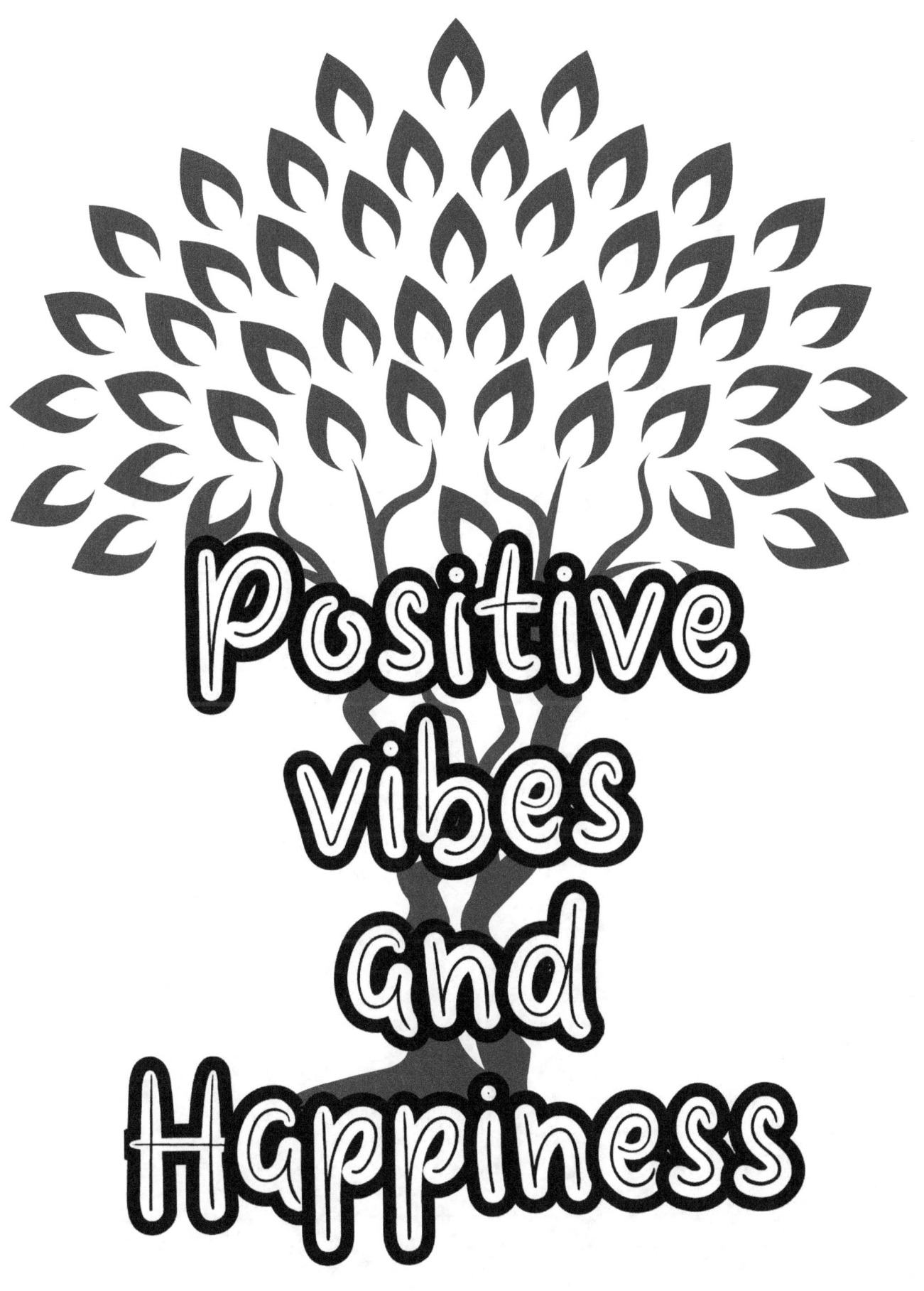

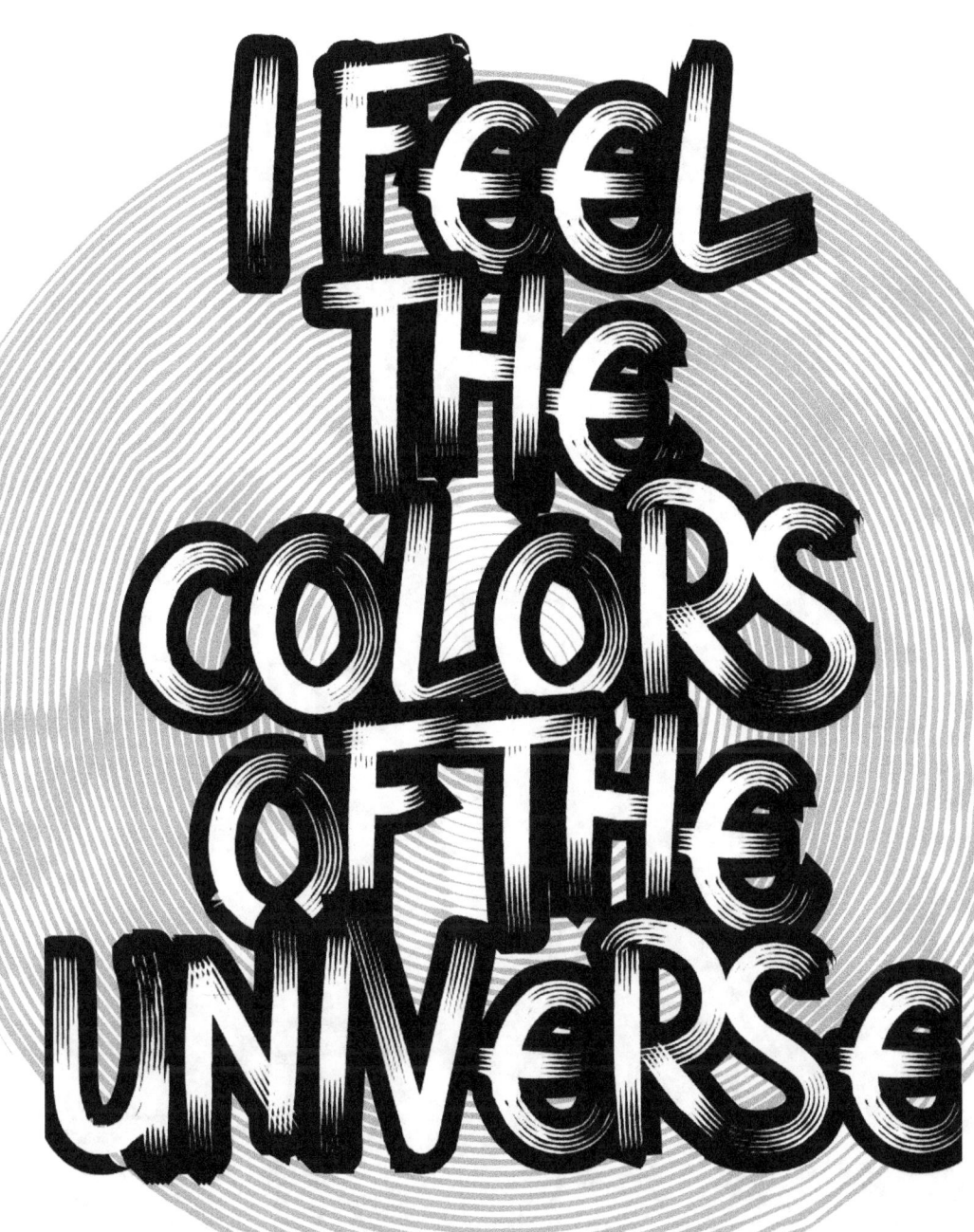

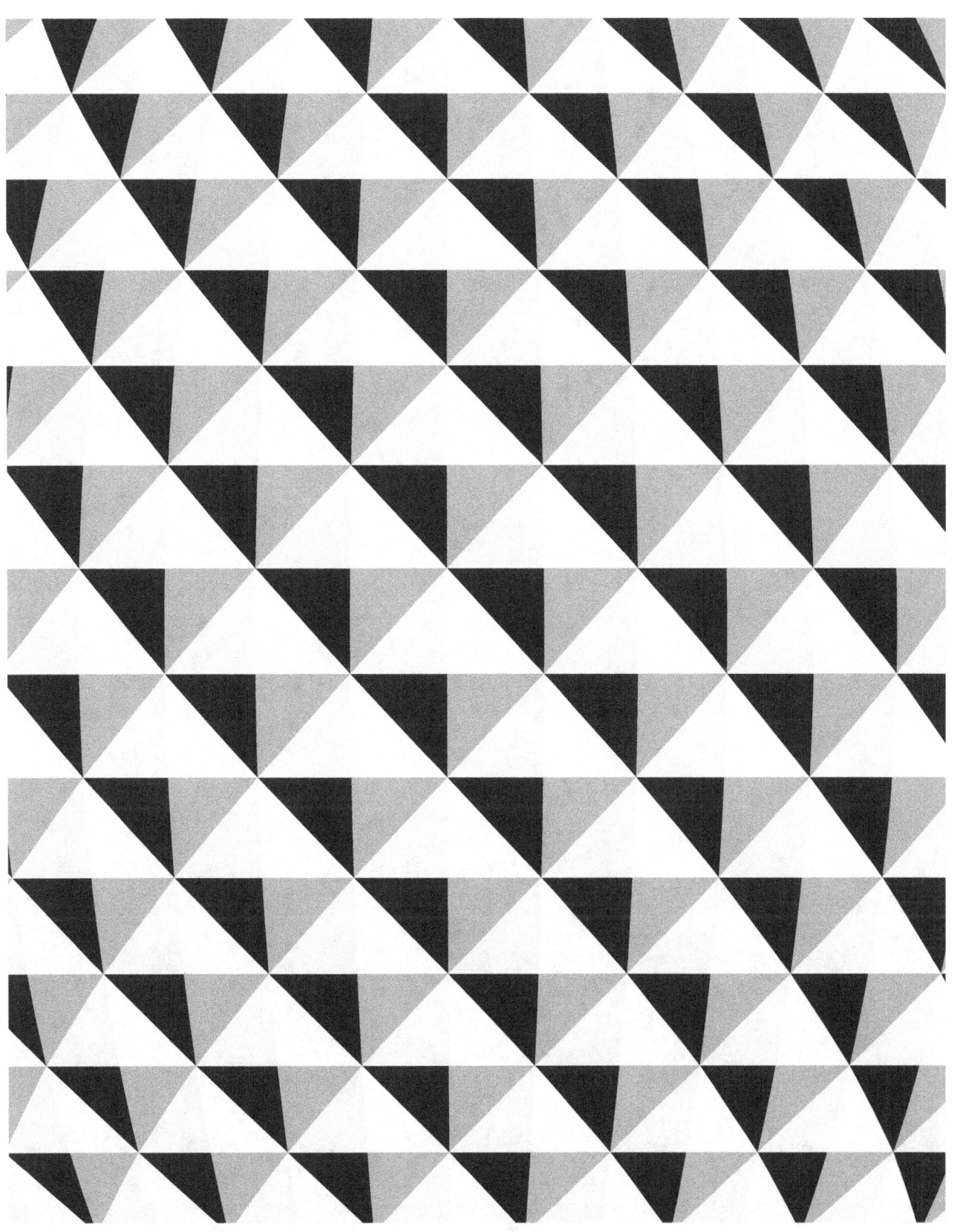

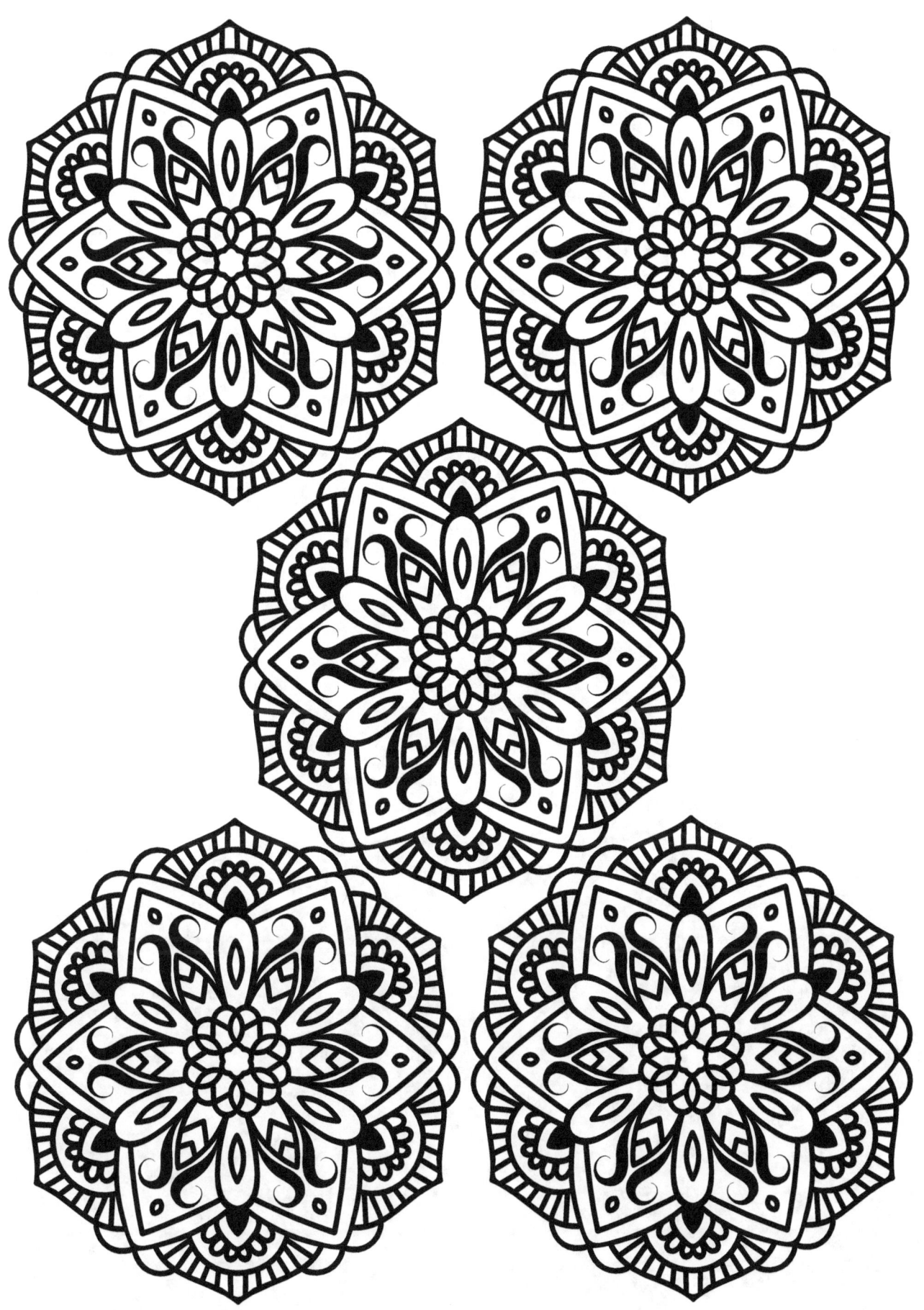

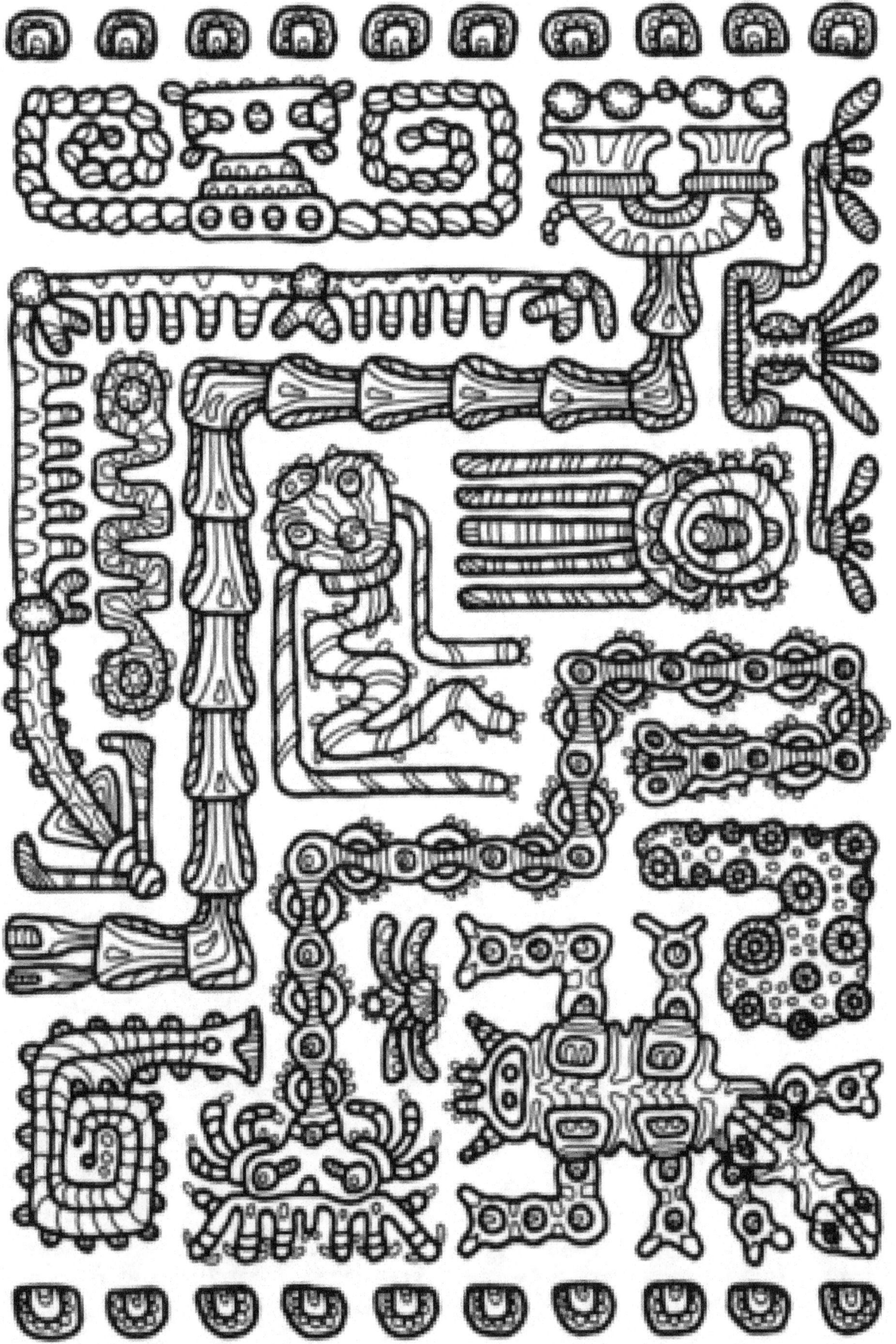

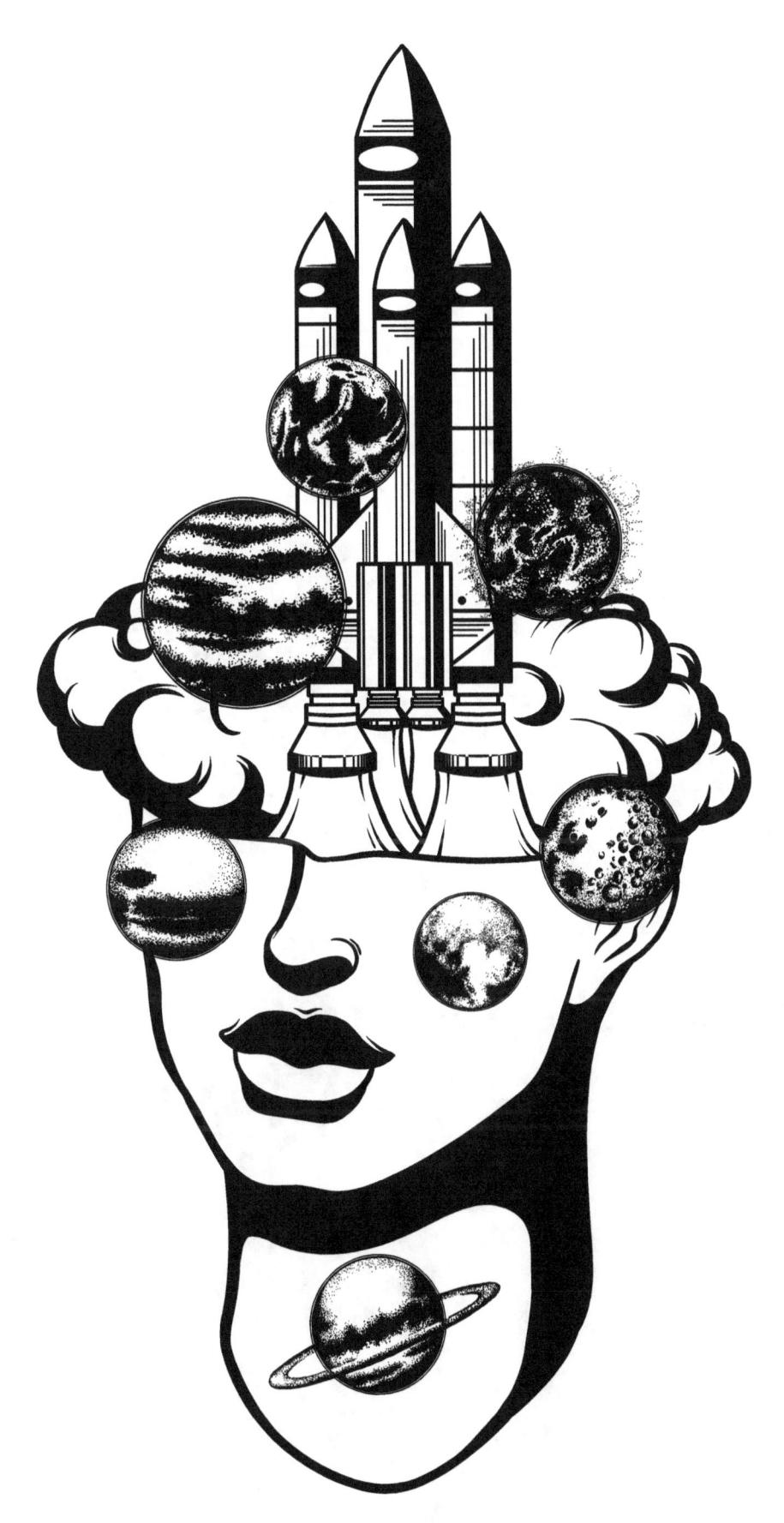

THE MORE YOU CARE THE MORE YOU LOOSE

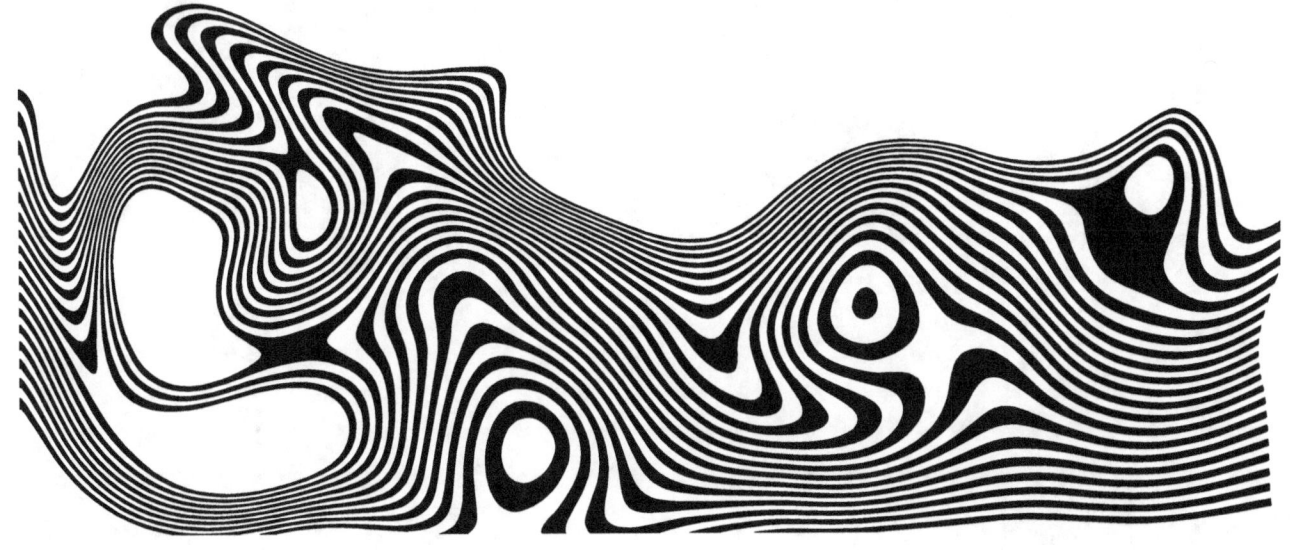

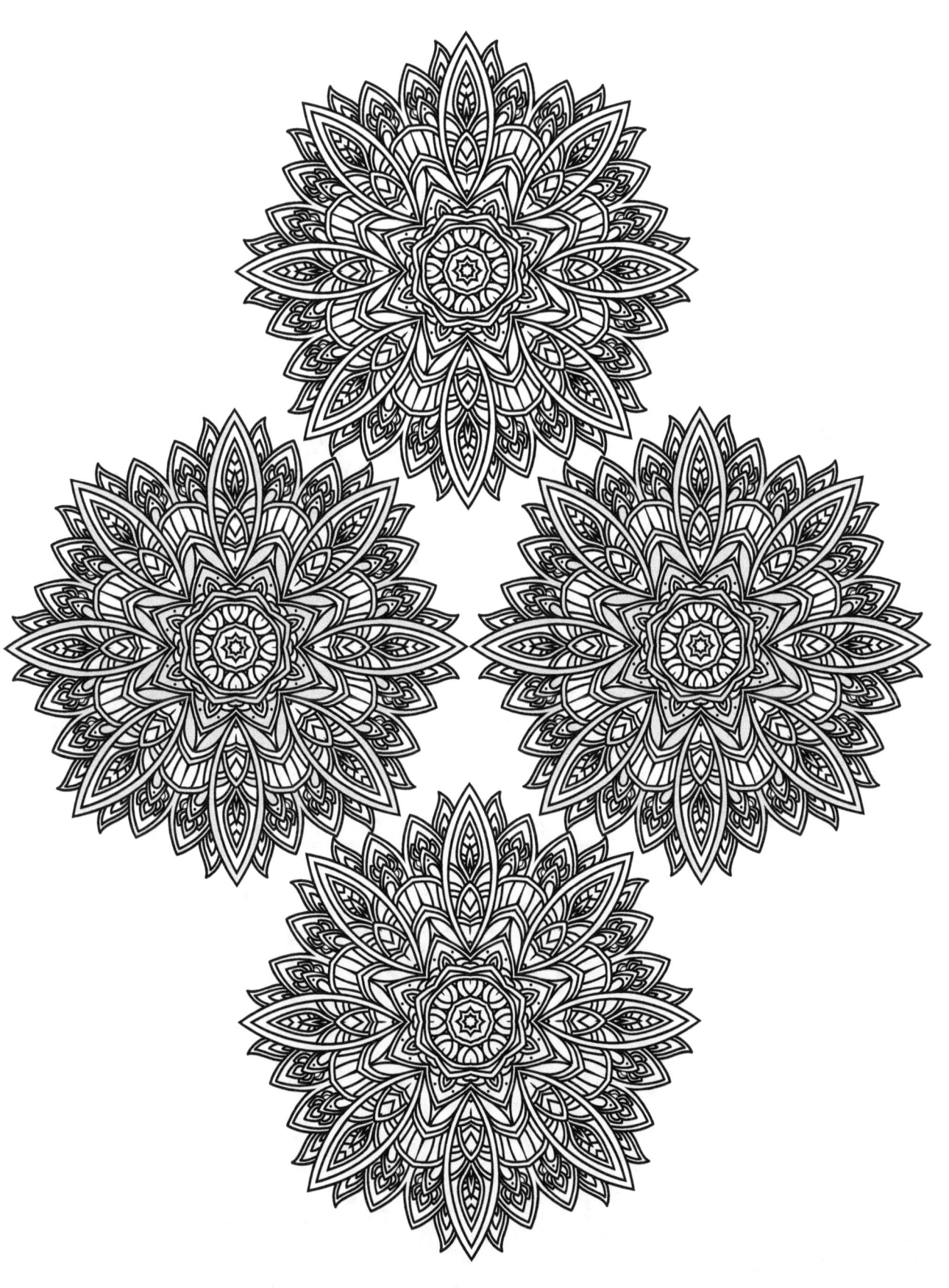

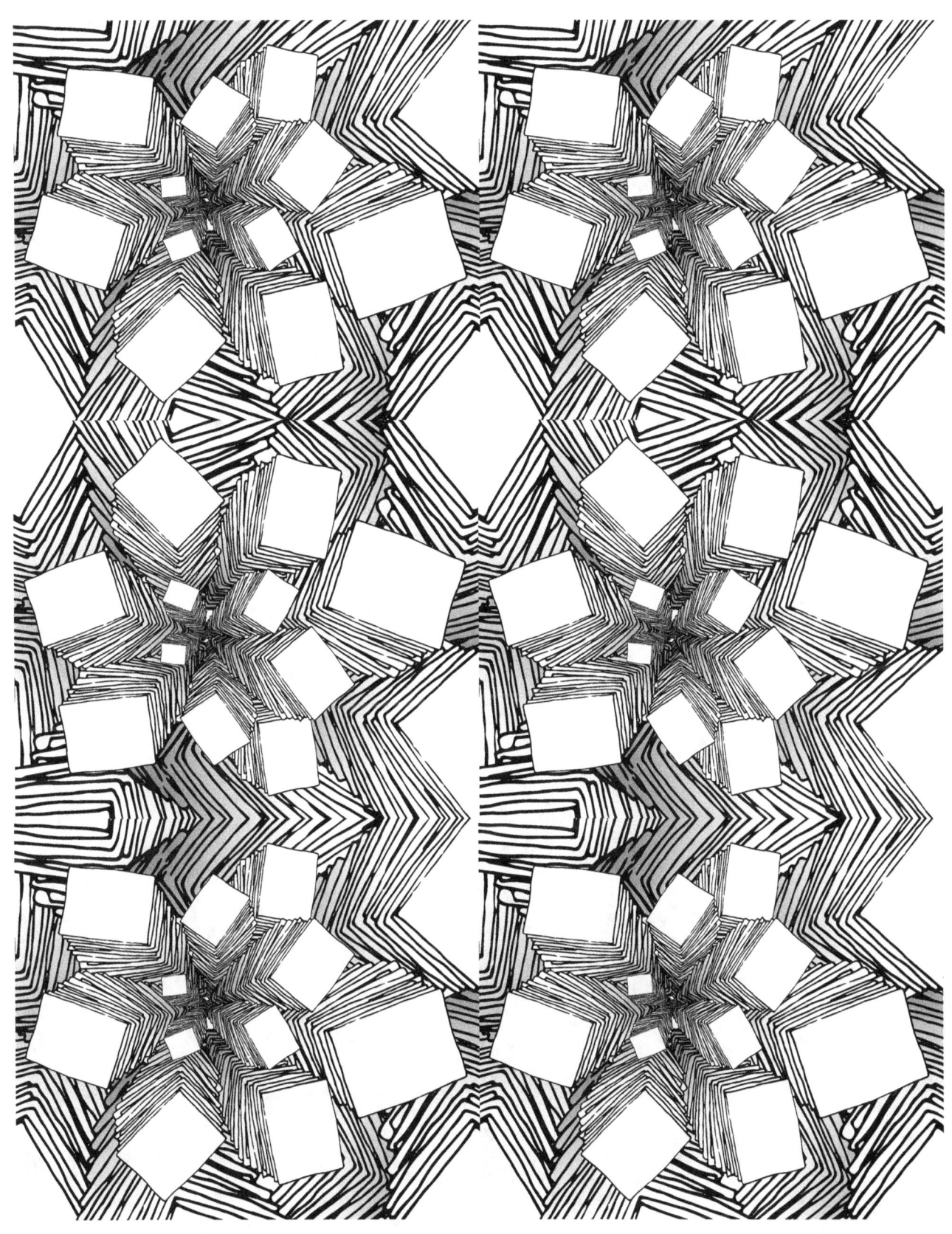

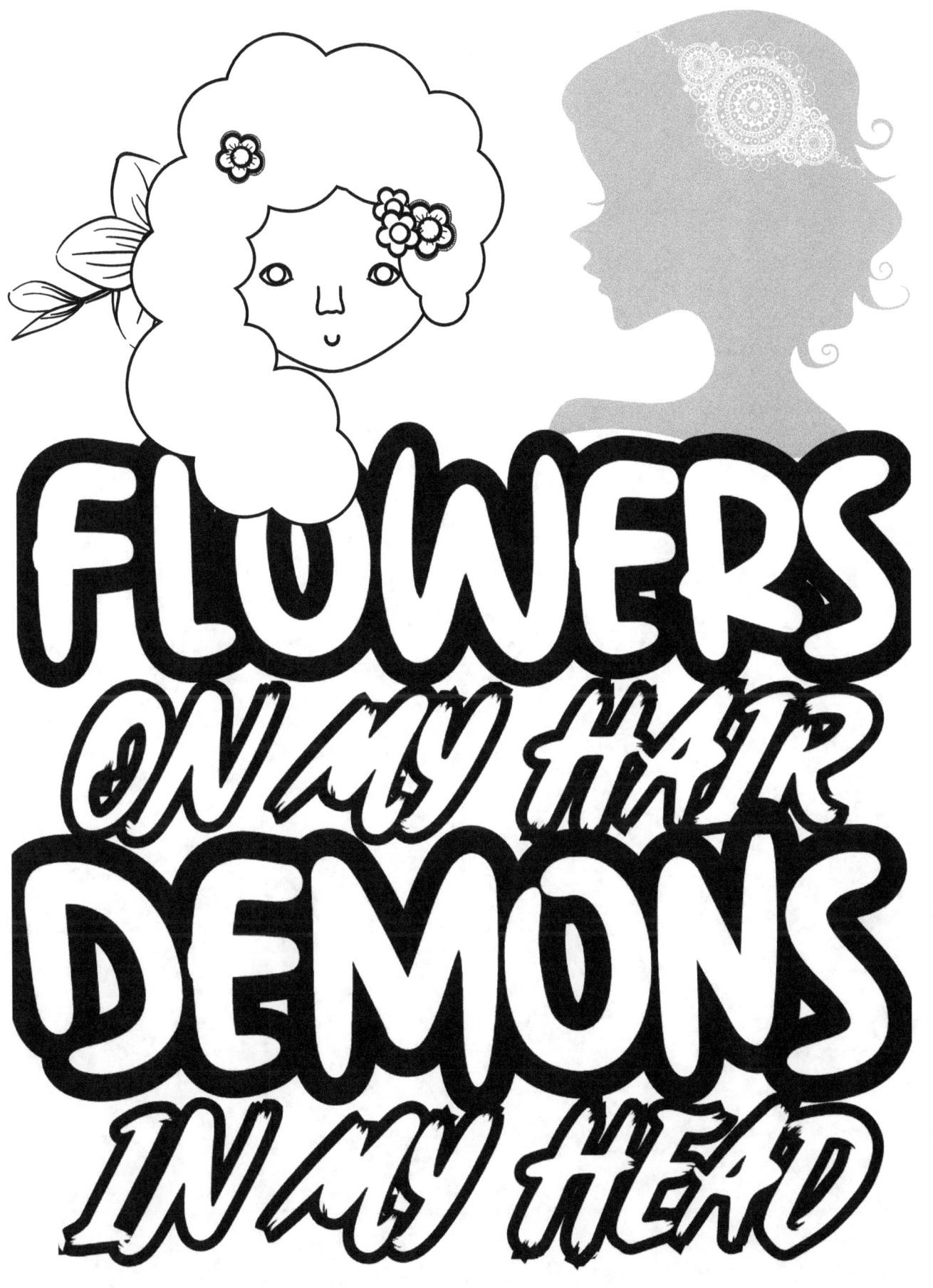

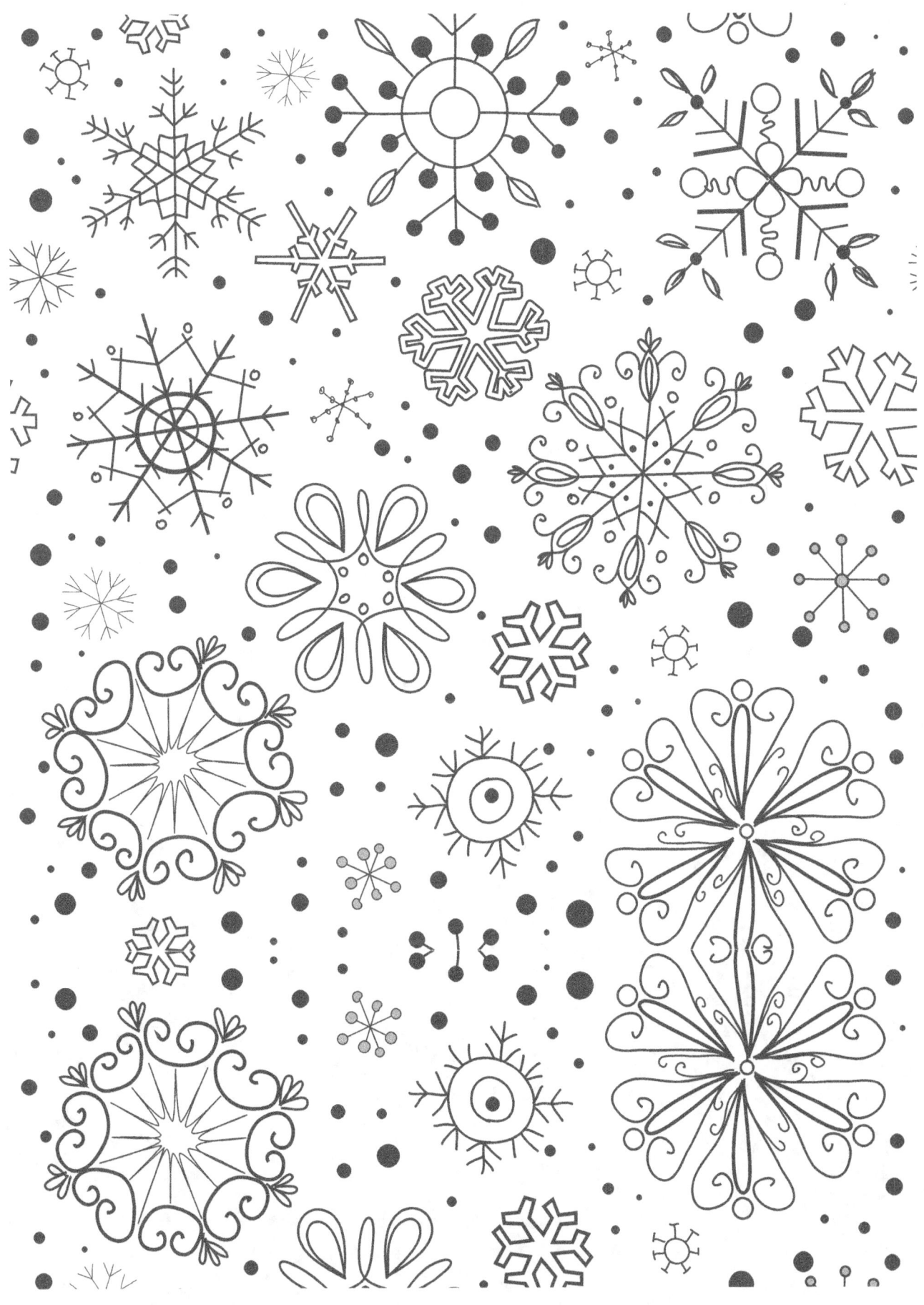

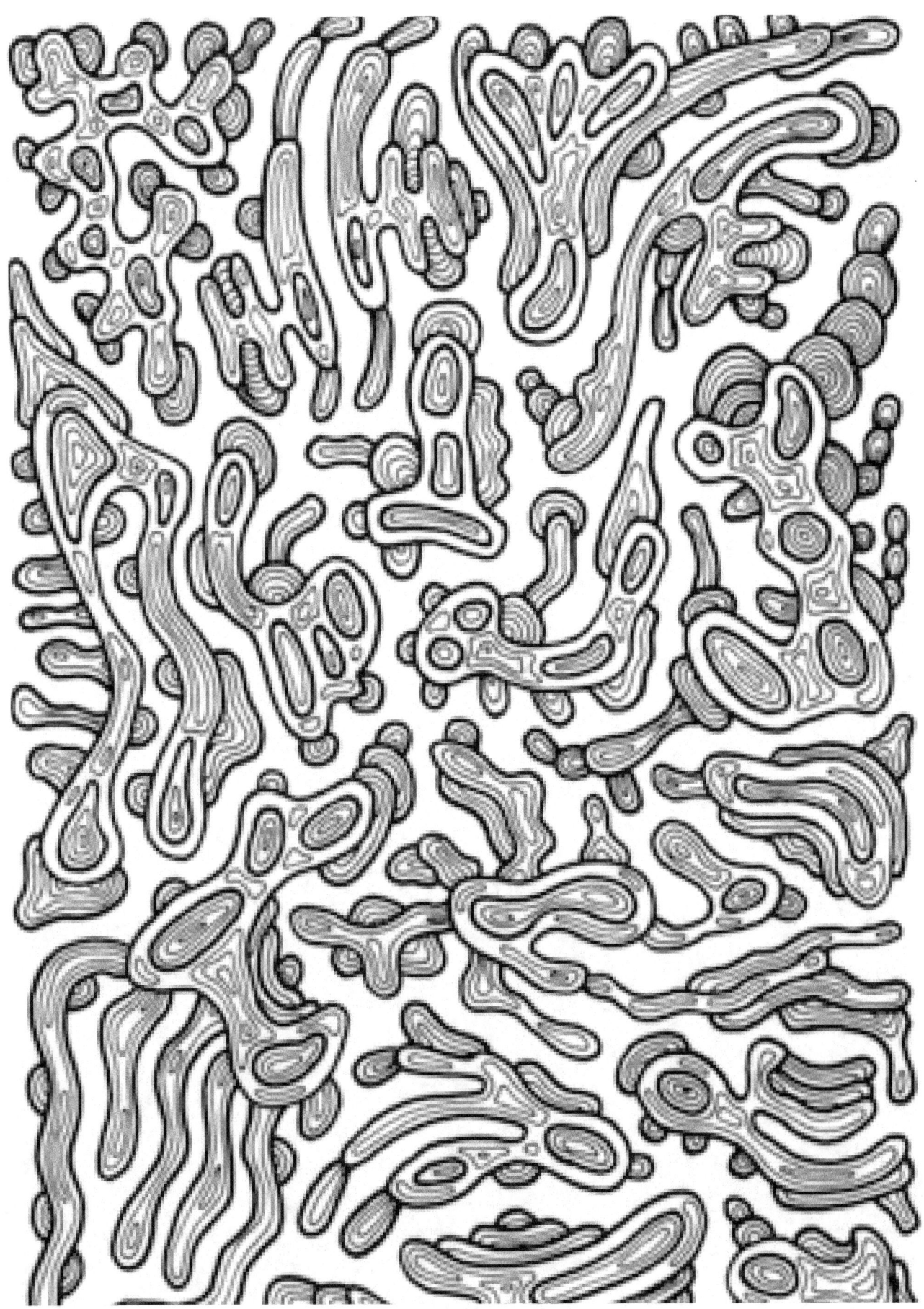

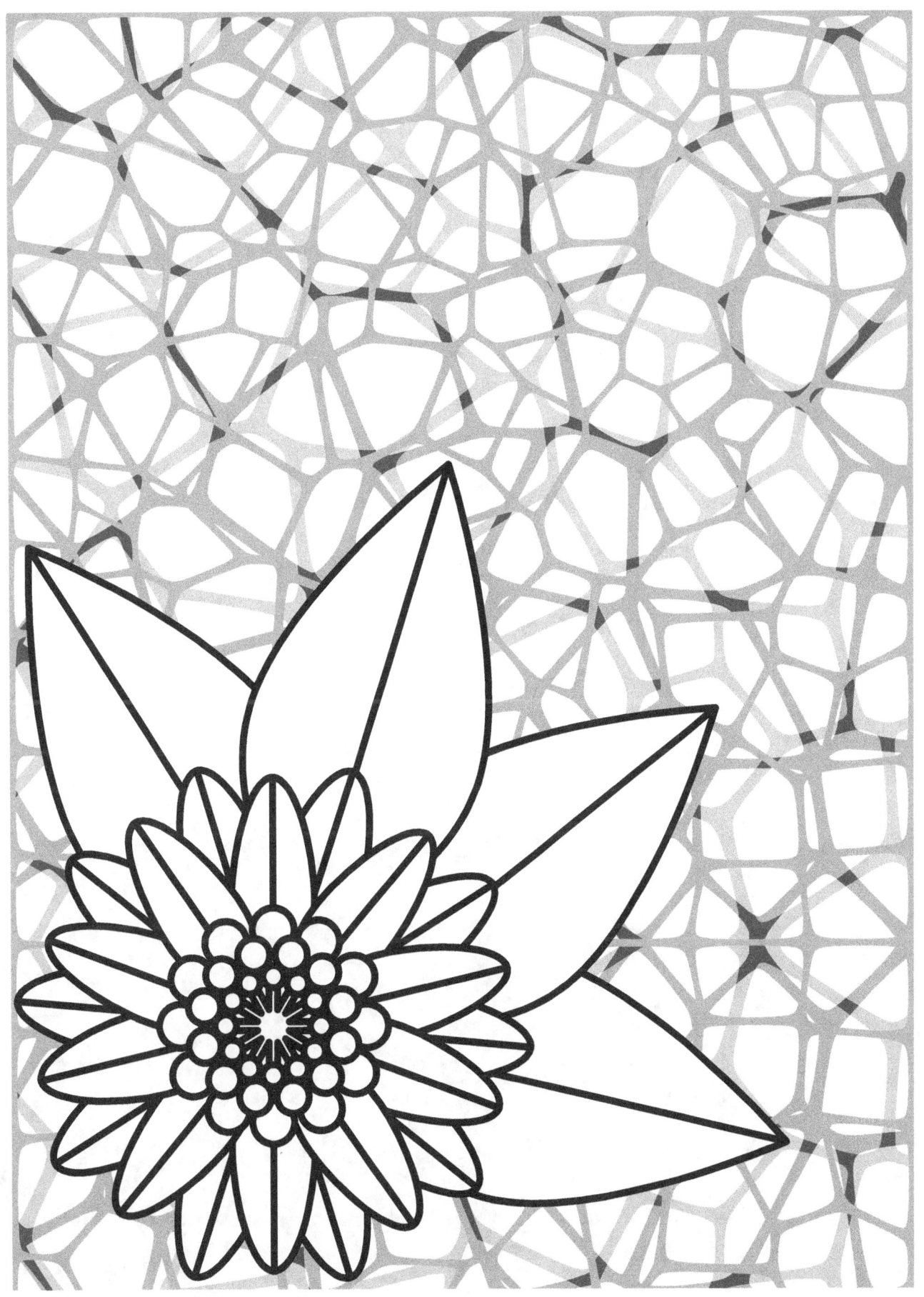

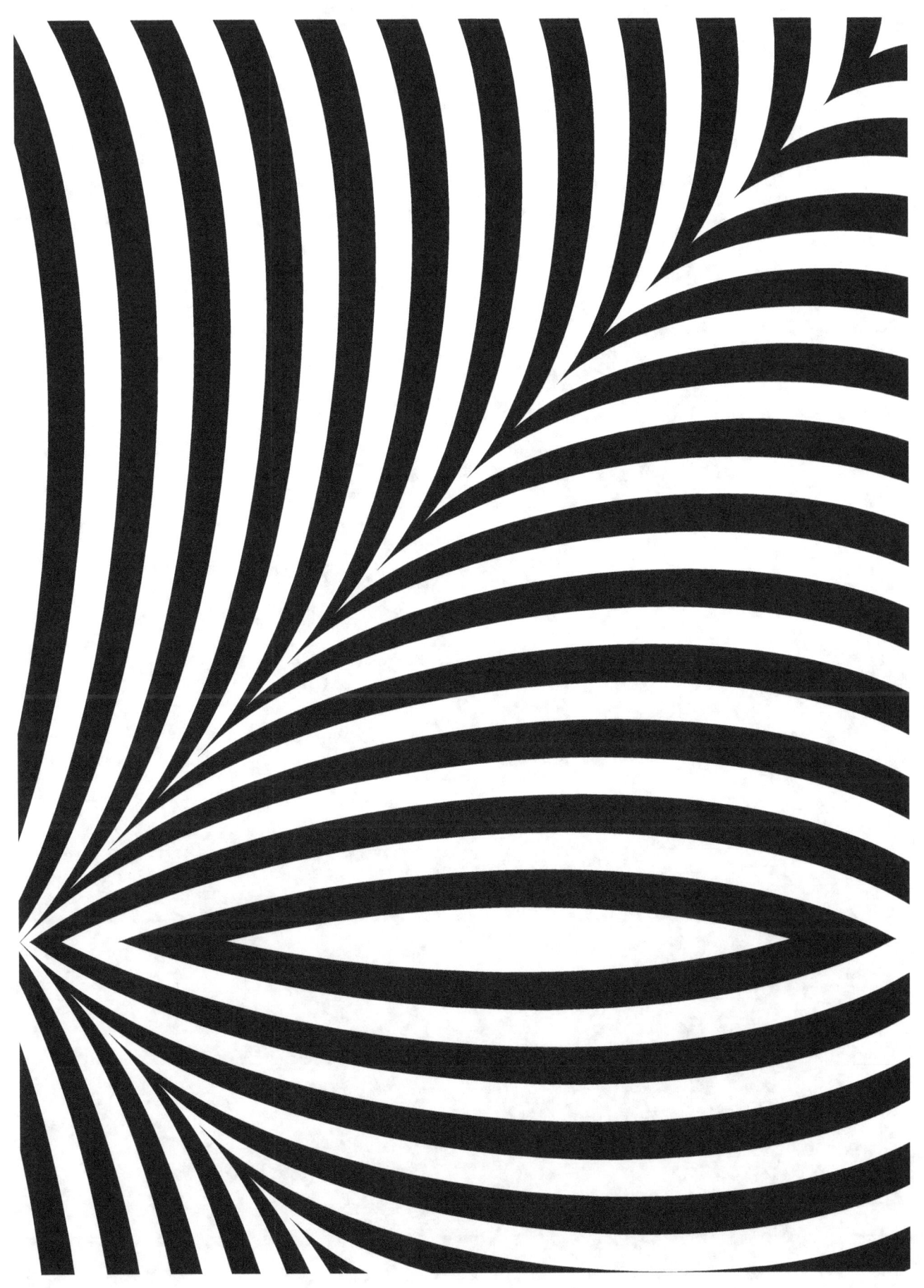

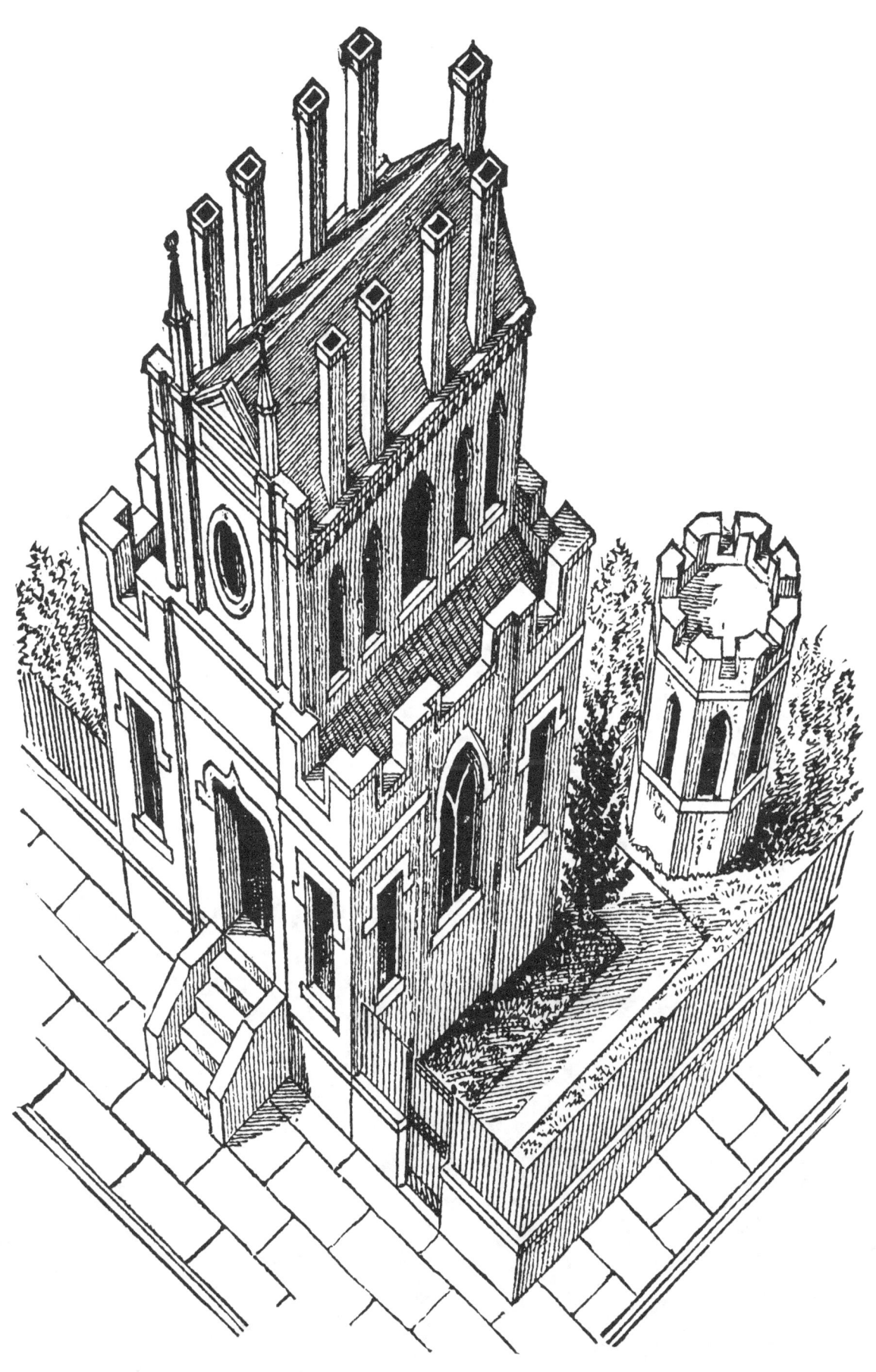

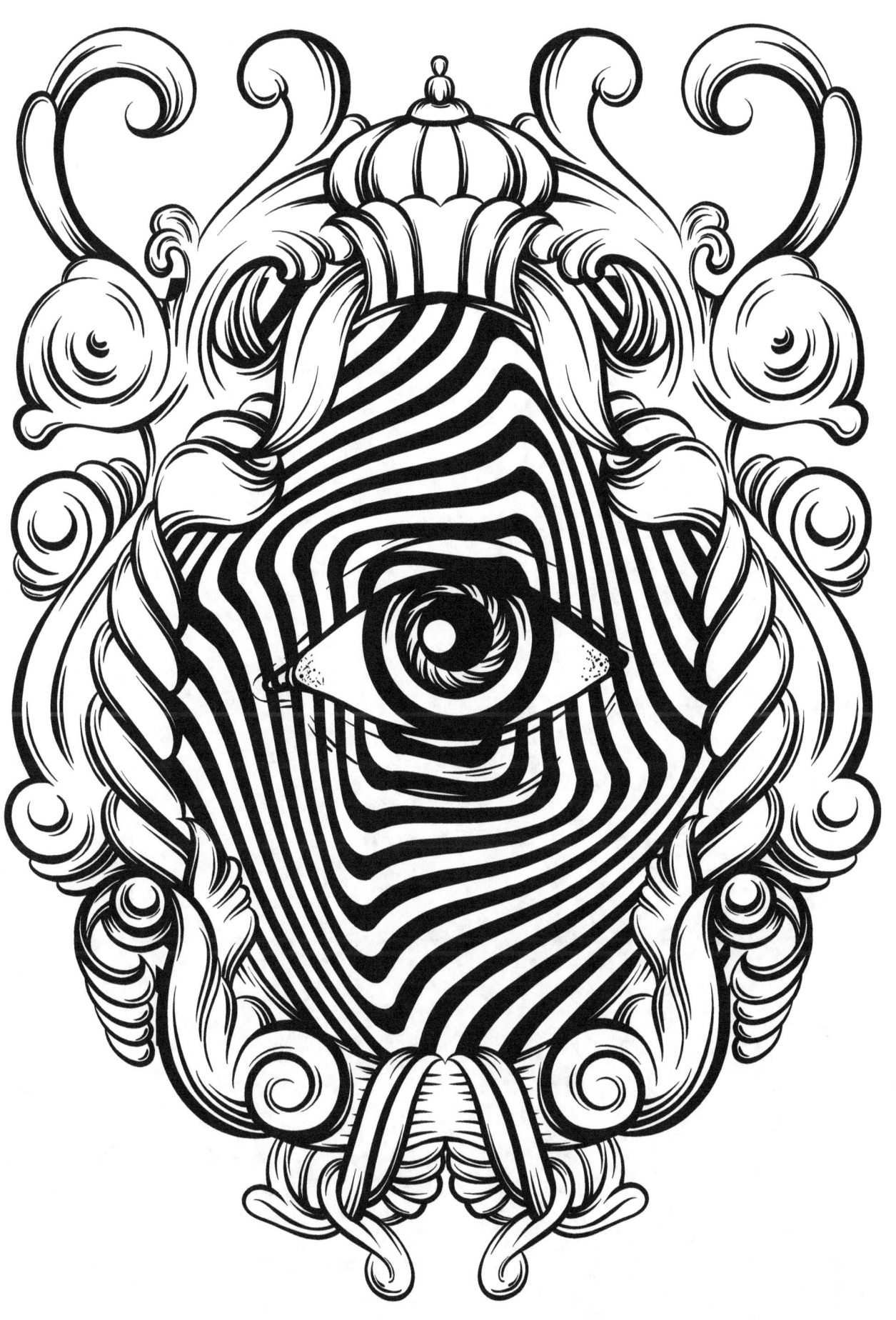

Think Free Live Free

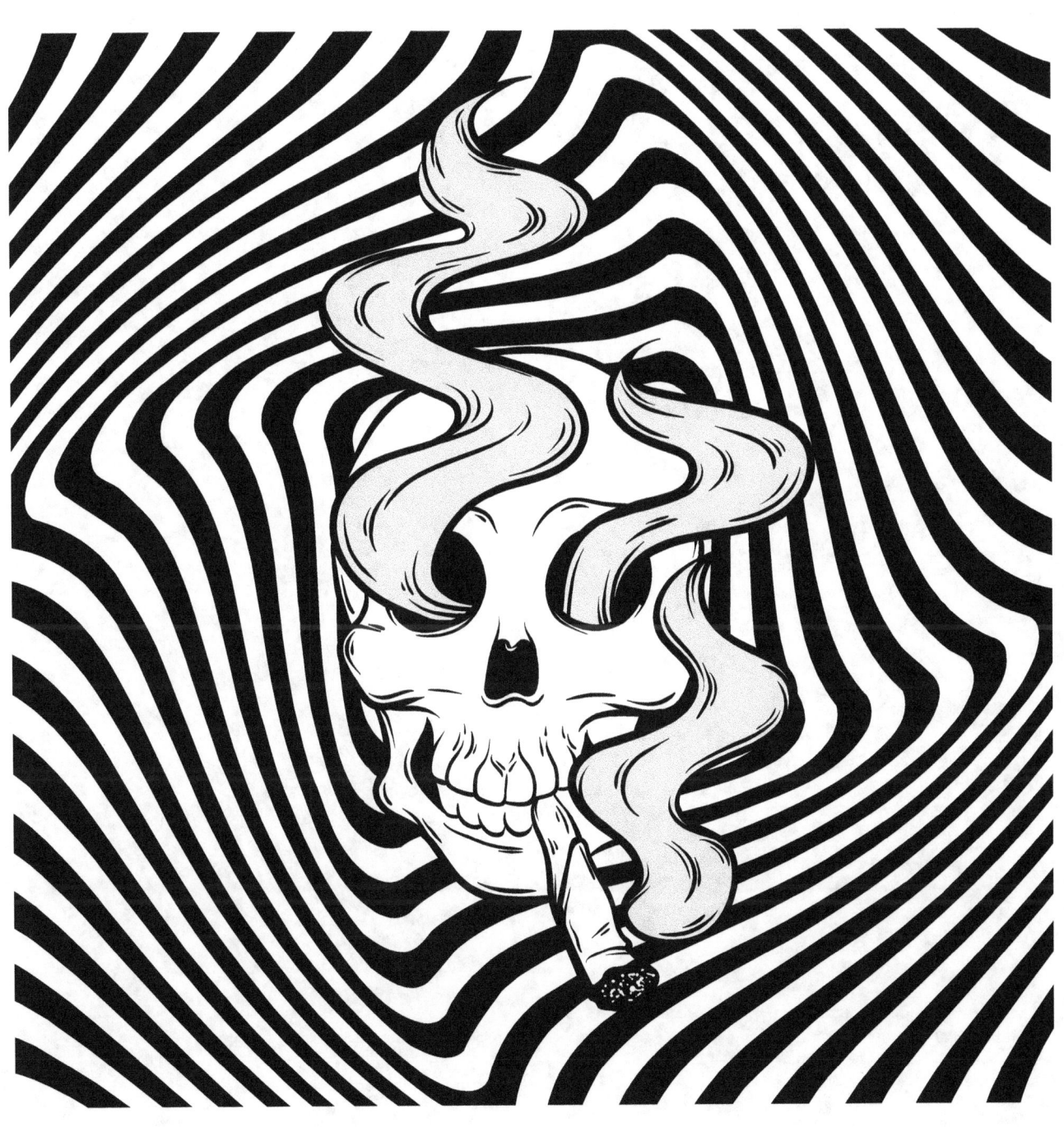

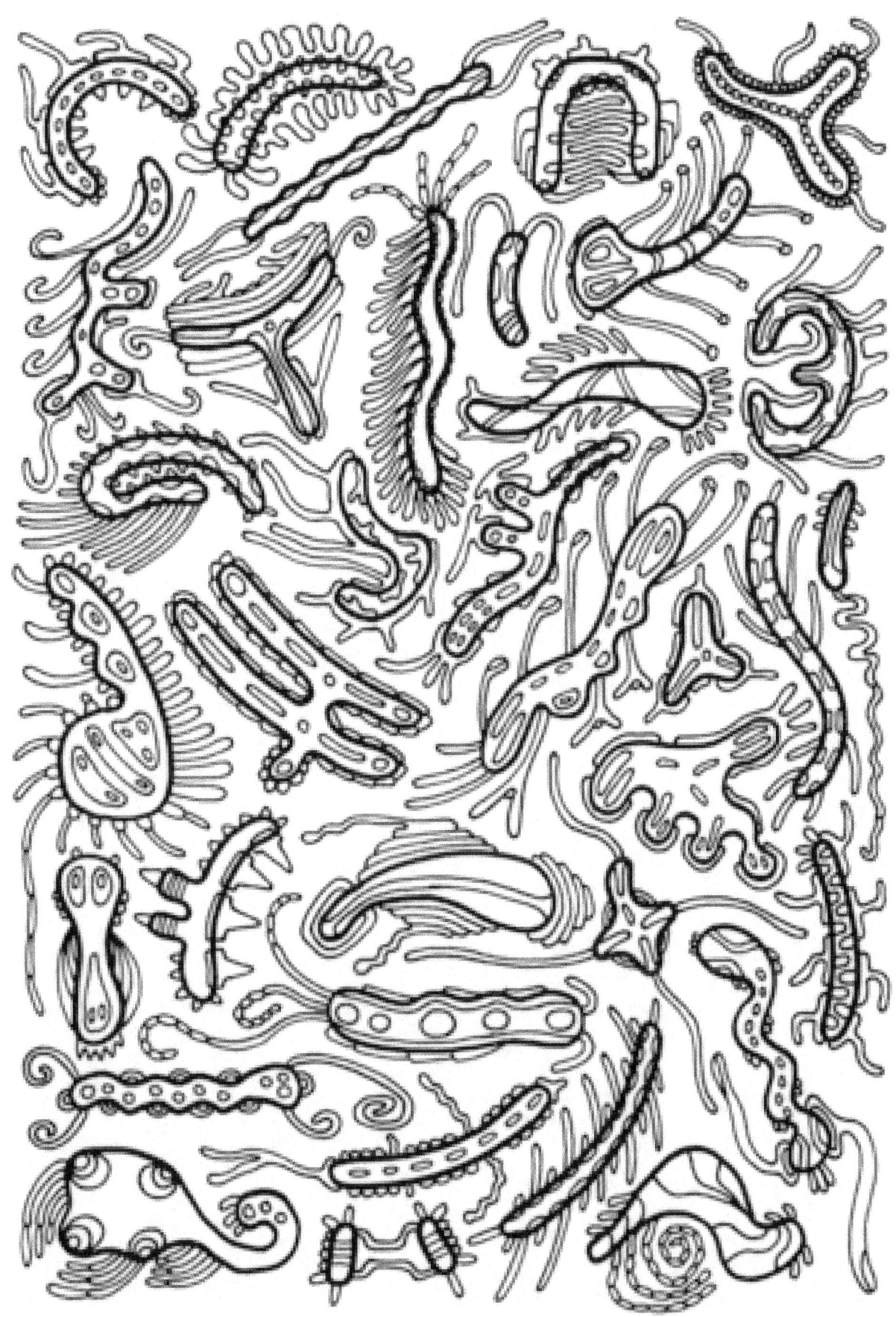

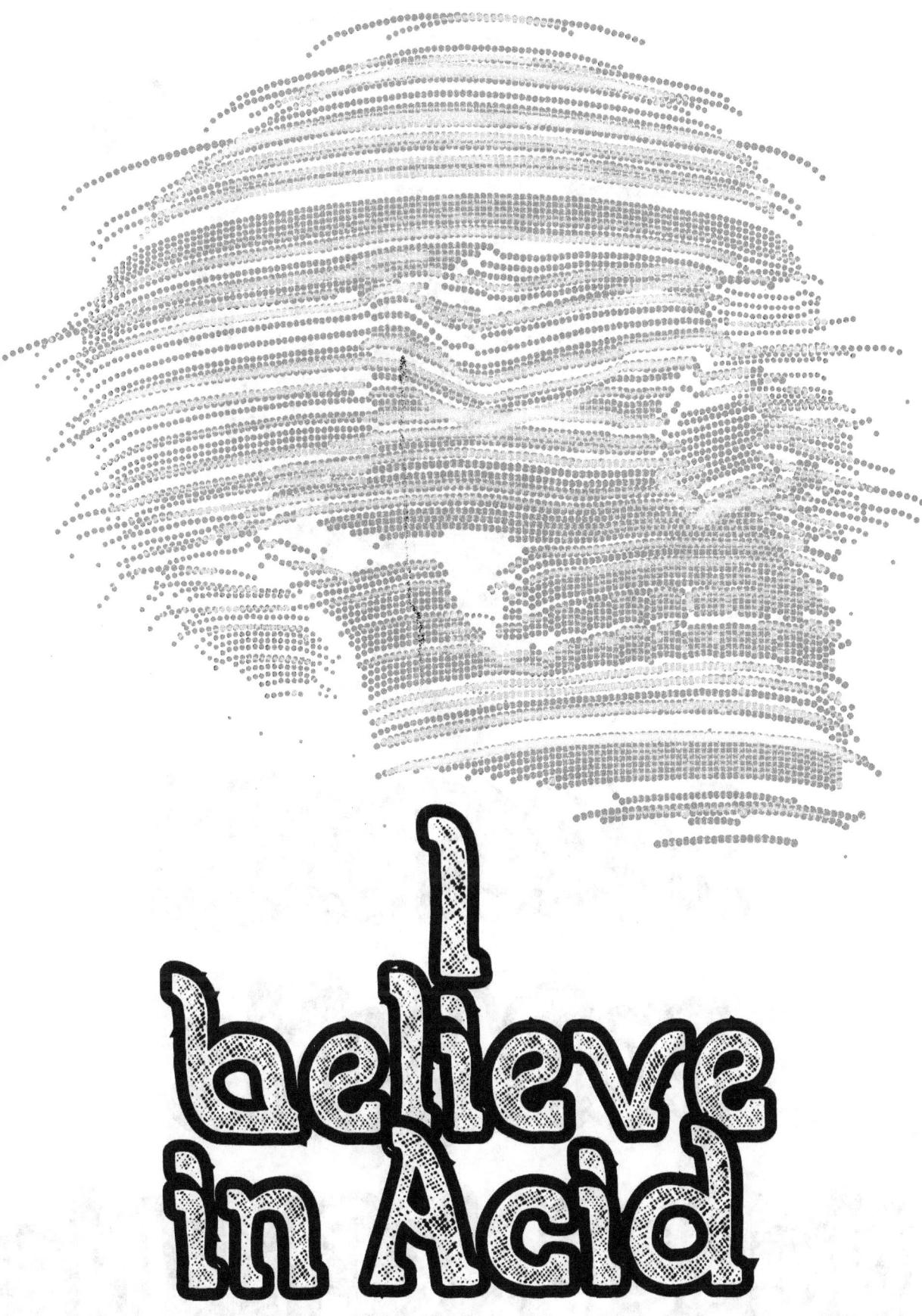

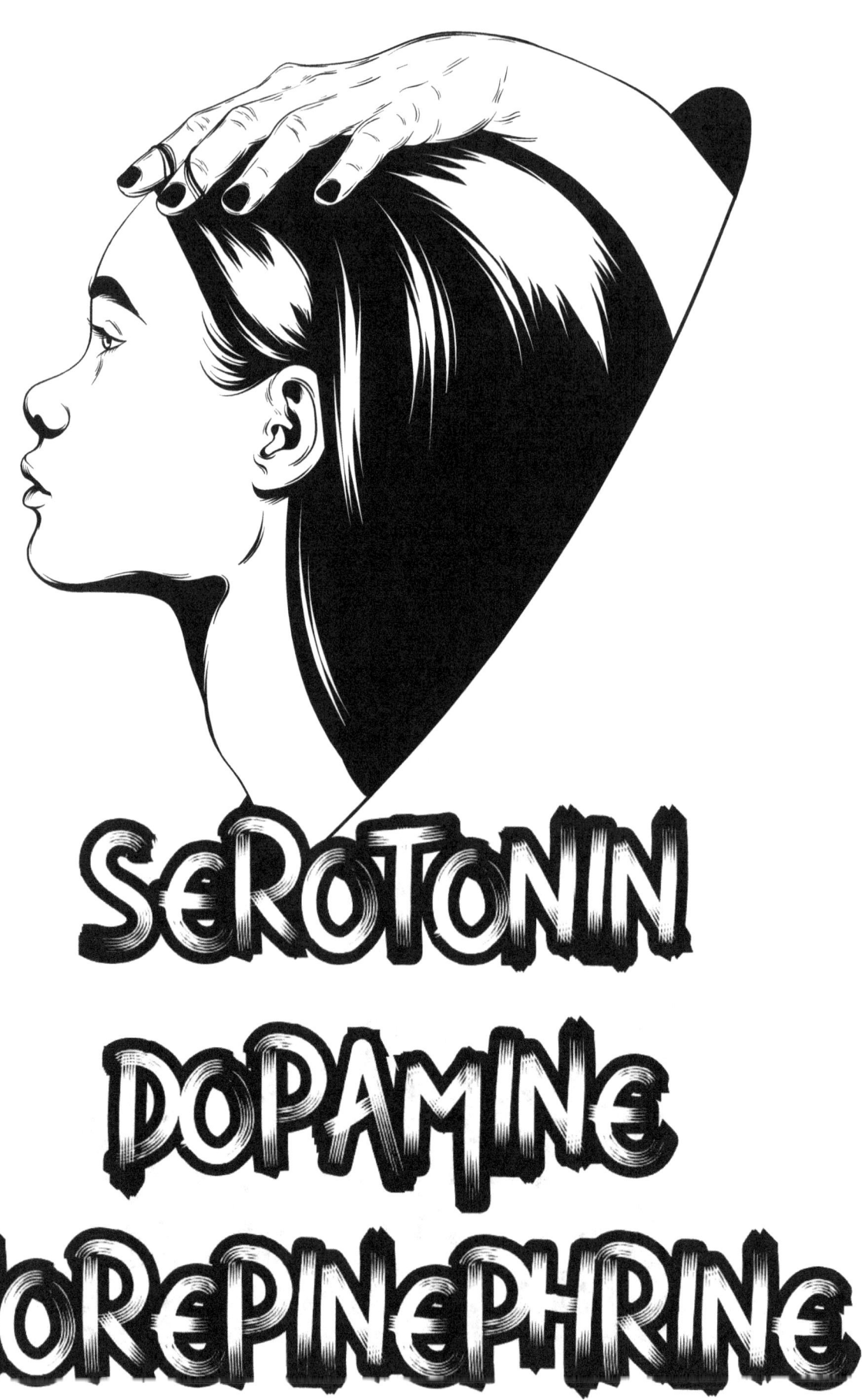

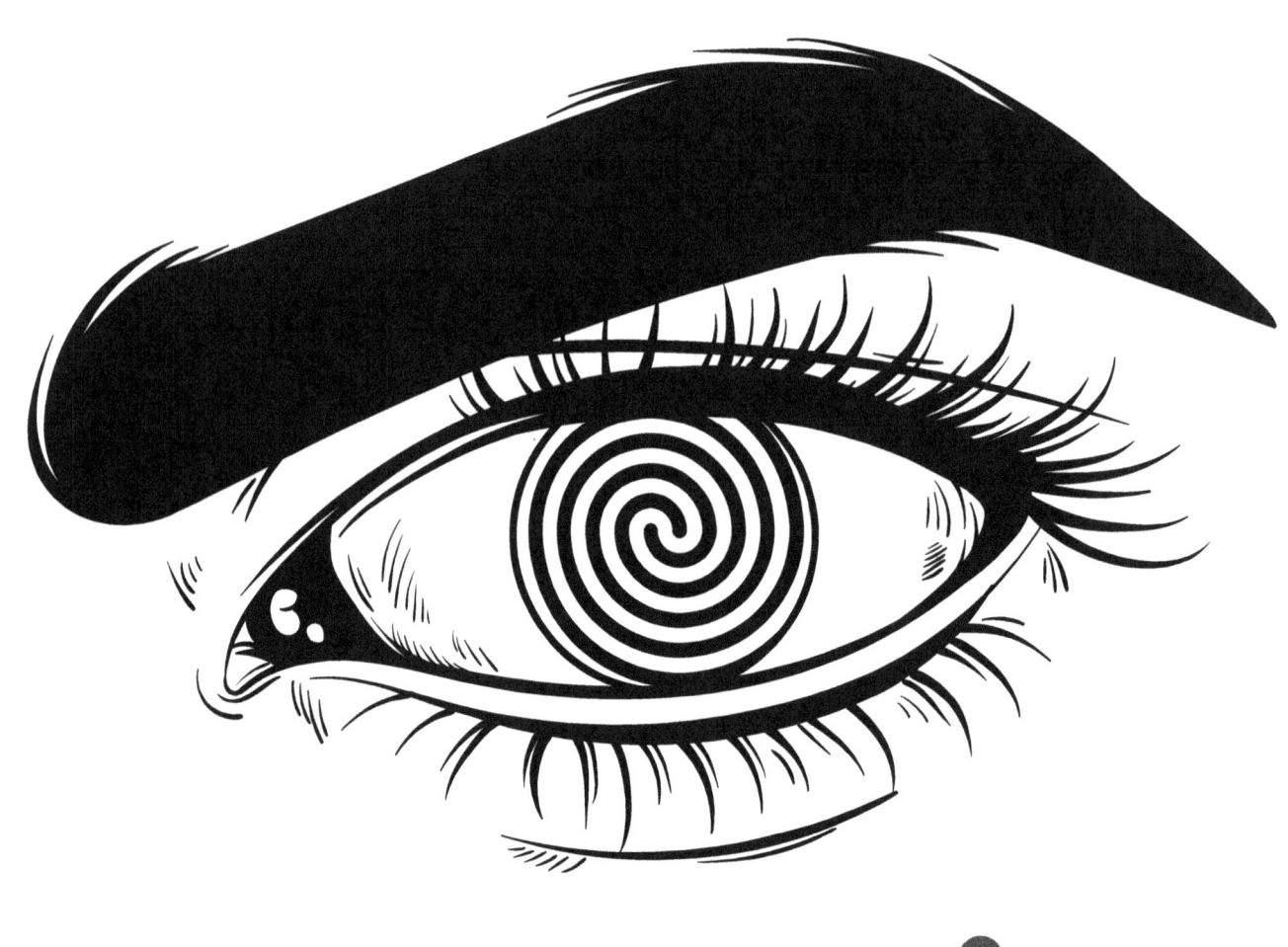